Wild Derbyshire

Paul Hobson

Photographs, words and design by Paul Hobson

Copyright © 2012 Paul Hobson

www.paulhobson.co.uk

No part of this publication may be reproduced, stored in a retrieval system or transmitted in any form or by any means without prior permission of the author.

ISBN: 978-0-9570265-1-3

Natures Images Publishing

Printed on FSC certified paper

A seven-spot ladybird takes to the air in Padley Woods.
Great crested grebes grace many of Derbyshire's waters ▶

Wild Derbyshire

Derbyshire sits perfectly in the heart of England and its wildlife reflects not only this position but also its diverse geology and topography. Wild moorlands resound to the calls of red grouse whilst the nimble paws of mountain hares bound for the horizon. Goshawks quietly patrol valley woodlands and buzzards and red kites wheel in the air above.

Ospreys fish rivers and reservoirs and it must only be a short time before they breed. Otters have re-colonised many of the river systems where water voles, Britain's fastest declining mammal, still have healthy colonies. Clean, sparkling limestone-fed rivers cut into delightful dales where masses of early purple orchids overwhelm our senses in spring. In the north beautiful oak woods with singing pied flycatchers contrast with some of England's finest ash woods in the south.

The mighty Trent runs across the south of Derbyshire where recent gravel workings have been turned into superb nature reserves with breeding wetland birds, butterflies and dragonflies.

Derbyshire contains the bulk of Britain's first National Park, the Peak District. In the minds of many people the two are the same thing but this is far from the truth because this county has so much more to offer.

This is one of Britain's finest wildlife counties and this book aims to celebrate its great diversity and beauty. There have been many changes in the last ten years with far-reaching new conservation initiatives. We have lost some species. Red squirrels no longer catch our eye in the conifer woods, small blue butterflies have disappeared and our native crayfish is struggling. However, the ultimate tonic to these losses is Derby's cathedral dwelling peregrines and the return of Britain's most elegant flower, the lady's-slipper orchid and black grouse to our moorland fringes. What a county!

Throughout the book you will meet a selection of individuals, I have named them Derbyshire Custodians. I hope these will give a small reflection of the great diversity of people who work in Derbyshire who care for, have a keen interest in and passion for its wildlife.

Paul Hobson

Monk's Dale's mysterious, mossy woodlands.

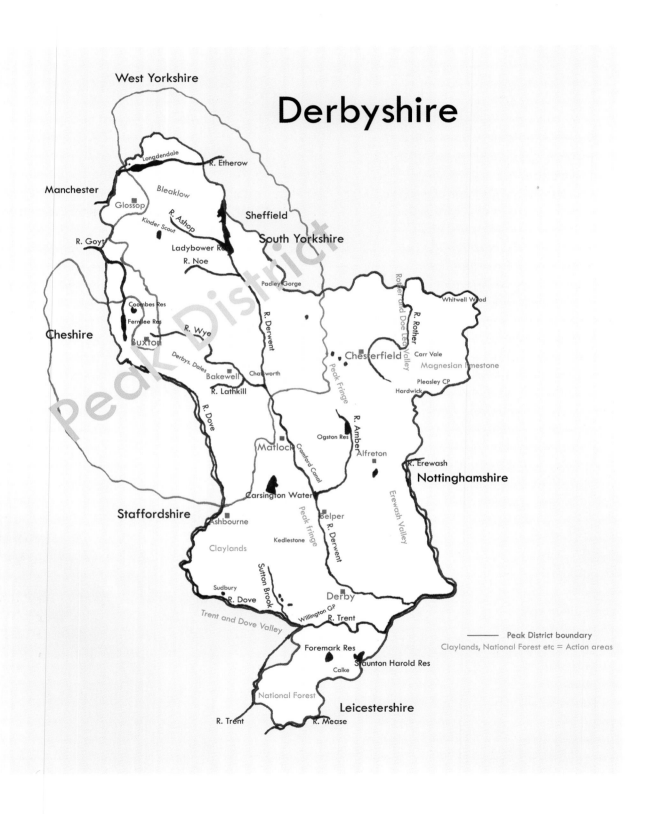

Derbyshire

Land-locked, Derbyshire is bordered to the east by Nottinghamshire, the south-east by Leicestershire, the west by Staffordshire and Cheshire, the north-west by Greater Manchester and the north-east by West and South Yorkshire.

Stunning scenery ranges from the wind-swept uplands of the north via the enchanting limestone dales to the flat, agriculturally productive lands in the south of the county. Much is incredibly beautiful countryside which was recognised by a major part being included in the UK's first national park, the Peak District, in 1951. In the south-east lies an area of industrialisation built on steel, coal mining and textiles.

Derbyshire's two significant rivers are the Trent, which runs across the south of the county, and the Derwent, which drains the north and runs south to Derby where it joins the Trent. There are many other smaller rivers, though probably none as attractive as the River Dove as it winds its way through gorgeous Dove Dale.

The county town is Derby, one of Britain's youngest cities, having been given Royal Charter in 1977. Other significant towns include Alfreton, Ashbourne, Bakewell, Buxton, Chesterfield, Glossop and Matlock.

Derbyshire has long been moulded by the hand of man and some of England's earliest human archaeology is found at the world famous Creswell Crags on the Derby-Nottingham border. Here our early ancestors hunted and dined on rhino and hippo, clear evidence that the climate and landscape were very different long ago. There are numerous Bronze Age burial mounds and magical stone circles such as Arbor Low near Buxton. The Romans left their calling card with roads, old lead mine workings and the beginnings of Buxton.

At one time part of the Anglo-Saxon kingdom of Mercia, Derbyshire later became part of Danelaw, named after the Danes who established the town of Derby. The name of Derbyshire was first noted in 1049 as Deorbyscir, a Danish term for Derby and its surrounding lands.

Agriculture dominated until the 17th century when iron ore was first exploited, helping the early growth of the steel and engineering industry around the south east of the county. These industries expanded during the 18th and 19th centuries when coal mining also helped to shape the land.

Derbyshire had an influential hand in the inception of the factory system with Sir Richard Arkwright's water-powered silk mill at Cromford in 1771. This was Britain's first factory and now has World Heritage status. Other famous companies also grew up, such as Rolls Royce in Derby.

Today the county is dominated by the Peak District National Park with tourism playing a significant part in its economic well-being. The south of Derbyshire is still a major employer in the engineering field, though coal mining has declined dramatically since the 1980's. Quarrying is still present with Europe's largest limestone quarry found near Buxton. Other minerals either mined now or in the past include dolomite, sand, gravel, fluorspar, lead, clay and coal. In fact Derbyshire can be claimed to be Britain's mineral capital.

Agriculture is the dominant land use from the Derbyshire Gritstone sheep of the rugged moors to the grain, grass and dairy of the south.

Over the last 600 years Derbyshire has been the home of some of Britain's most rich, famous and influential personalities. None have been more impressive than Bess of Hardwick (1521-1608) and her legacy of Hardwick Hall is one of the realm's most stunning Elizabethan houses. Izaak Walton (1593-1683) leisurely fished the River Dove and penned the fisherman's bible, The Complete Angler. Florence Nightingale (1820-1910) who worked tirelessly in the Crimean conflict is a Derbyshire daughter and Henry Royce (1863-1933) established Rolls Royce at Derby. Later DH Lawrence (1885-1930) and Thomas Cook (1808-1892) established themselves as leaders in their fields of literature and global travel.

Derbyshire has a number of its own unique customs with two being of particular note - well dressing and Shrovetide football. Well dressing has existed as a form of decorating the heads of wells from pagan times. The oldest known well dressing was at Tissington in 1349. Today over 50 well dressings occur each year. Shrovetide football possibly has its beginnings over 1000 years ago. Taking place at Ashbourne each year up to 10,000 players maul and ruck for two days in a pitched battle!

No mention of Derbyshire would be complete without a comment on the world famous Bakewell tart, or pudding, depending on which story you believe. Created in two different bakeries these satisfy the hunger of thousands of locals and tourists each year.

Derbyshire has been shown many times on TV. Peak Practice was set here as was The League of Gentleman. Many of the county's finest houses have attracted the attentions of film and TV with recent productions of Pride and Prejudice at Chatsworth and Jane Eyre at Haddon Hall.

The thousands of visitors to Derbyshire who come to walk and relax in the wilds of the Peak often spend some time visiting some of its stunning buildings and homes. Pride of place must go to Chatsworth which is possibly Britain's best loved Country House. Chatsworth and its vast estate is the seat of the Duke of Devonshire (Cavendish family) and home to some of the county's oldest veteran trees. Eyam Hall in the plague village of Eyam dates from 1671 and Haddon Hall on the lovely River Wye from the 14th century. Hardwick Hall was the home of Bess and further south is found Kedleston Hall which was built for Sir Richard Curzon between 1759 and 1765.

A brown hare runs across a Claylands field in spring ▶

Woodland Derbyshire

After the last glacial period the forests started to get their roots firmly embedded into the soil of Britain. Our first forest was dominated by birch and Scots pine around 8000 years ago. Then the climate became damper and areas of peat bog started to form in upland areas. By 500 BC Derbyshire's natural vegetation type was ash or oak forest bisected by river valleys with areas of bog on the treeless uplands.

The wildlife was both familiar and exotic compared to today. Brown bears and wolves hunted alongside early humans and any meetings must have done a little more than raise the hairs on the back of the neck! Birdlife was probably close to what we find now along with familiar mammals such as hedgehogs and badgers.

Forest clearance in Derbyshire started in the Neolithic and Bronze ages where small areas were cleared to grow crops or keep animals. The Romans did not markedly increase forest clearance but the Anglo-Saxons clearly sped up the process. Many Anglo-Saxon names bear woodland links - clough, den, hey and ley. Once the Normans had seen off Harold's army they set about recording and implementing Britain's first woodland protection. The introduction of Royal Forests was a clear attempt to manage the land, mainly for hunting. Peak Forest and Macclesfield Forest were hunted by the Normans for wild boar and red deer.

The Middle Ages saw forest clearance proceed unabated with fuel for lead smelting becoming a factor. By the 17th century most of the forest in Derbyshire had gone, though upland areas fared better for a while. In a few river valleys woodland did survive such as at Padley, one of the best examples of an upland oak wood in Derbyshire.

The 17th and 18th centuries saw real attempts at trying to increase Derbyshire's tree cover. Richard Arkwright planted 50,000 trees in the Wye valley. Joseph Paxton saw woodlands as important landscape features when he designed the parkland at Chatsworth and the 5th Duke of Rutland had similar views, planting thousands of trees on the Haddon estate, now tremendous, mature woodlands.

Conifer planting after the two great wars never really affected the moors of the Peak though some did occur following the creation of Ladybower reservoir. Here scots pine, sitka spruce and larch feature, with the latter bringing one of the county's finest autumn spectacles.

◄ Acorn weevil, National Forest.

The woodland floor has an important role to play in keeping the trees healthy. Many small invertebrates like snails browse woodland plants stopping them overrunning the forest. They also provide food for small mammals such as wood mice and birds such as song thrushes. How everything is interlinked and dependent on each other makes woodlands so dynamic and exciting.

Many of the woods were managed by coppicing. Using a rotational system the trees are cut back to the stump, known as a stool. In the following 15 to 20 years the trees put on an amazing spurt of growth and produce long, slender shoots which are ideal for handles for tools, basket making, fencing or charcoal production. The wildlife benefits are huge. Light floods the woodland floor and plants like wood anemone and common dog's violet bloom, increasing the presence of butterflies and birds of open scrub like the warblers. Because the system is rotational there are areas of different aged trees, each with a slightly different set of species. Today we call this biodiversity.

Woodland management today has to replace the effects of storms and natural fires which allowed trees to regenerate and create light-rich openings for woodland plants and butterflies. Dead wood now lies where it falls and benefits dozens of beetle species. Many of Derbyshire's woods aged but didn't regenerate because of sheep or deer and became dark as coppicing fell out of favour. Today the challenge is not only to increase the county's woodland coverage but also to manage the neglected woods both for the benefit of wildlife and areas for relaxation and recreation.

Today Derbyshire's woodland coverage is low, standing at 7.2% compared to the national average of 9%. Most woods are small though significant woodland coverage occurs in the Wye and Derwent valleys. The Derwent Valley (a World Heritage site) is one of the largest areas of connected woodland in the North of England and is very important nationally for woodland birds.

Approximately 78% of Derbyshire's woods are broad leafed with the remainder coniferous or mixed. This proportion has increased over the last 30 years and hopefully will continue to do so as active tree planting targets native species such as ash, oak and elm. Ecologists use the term 'ancient woods' which are woods known to have existed since 1600. As woods mature they slowly increase in plant biodiversity and this can give an idea about their age. A Forestry Commission survey in 2002 estimated that there are 44,000 hectares of ancient woodlands, which form 38% of the county's total woodland cover.

Woodland planting continues under a number of different schemes. In many former mining areas opportunities occur to create country parks, such as the one at Pleasley, where active tree planting occurs.

The Midlands of England have seen some of the worst aspects of industrial decline. Covering two hundred square miles of the Midlands, the National Forest is a landmark project rooted in the three counties of Derbyshire, Leicestershire and Staffordshire. It is not only an environmental scheme but one with many social and economic aspects as well. By 2009 woodland cover in this area had risen to a very respectable 18%, well on its way to its target of 30%.

In the north of Derbyshire upland woodlands mainly consist of sessile oak, together with both downy and silver birch, on slightly acidic soils. Dotted around are rowan (mountain ash), with its important red berries in late summer, and holly, once an important fodder crop. Where there are clearings and sheep have been excluded heather and bilberry will sprout

Old trees, particularly veterans, are full of holes which make great
places for bats, like this noctule, to roost or hibernate in.

vigorously. As the woods lose altitude bluebells start to appear alongside stitchwort and yellow archangel. Bluebells are important because Britain has 20% of the world total. Upland woodland birds are represented by pied flycatchers (below), wood warblers and redstarts.

Where a stream or water table is near the surface the soil is often waterlogged and here carrs, wet woodlands with alder and willow, develop. Wet carrs are important habitats in parts of the Dark Peak, the lower Derwent valley and on clays in the south of the county. Some important wet woodlands are found around lakes such as at Hardwick and Renishaw. The presence of alders in riverside areas helps the re-colonisation of Derbyshire by otters as the root complexes make safe places for their holts. Wet woodlands also provide an important habitat for many other species including marsh and willow tits, lesser-spotted woodpeckers and noctule bats.

Further south on the alkaline soiled limestone, ash is the main forest tree. As altitude increases ash slowly gives way to scrub with hazel and hawthorn becoming prominent, as in the woods in Miller's Dale, Ravensdale and Monk's Dale. In a few places globe flower can be found growing in damper patches and early spring sees superb displays of wood anemone, lesser celandine and dog's mercury carpeting the woodland floor. As summer progresses meadow and bloody cranesbills, water avens and violets bloom. Bird life is abundant here and the levels of a May dawn chorus can be deafening. Green woodpeckers 'yaffle' from the trees and hunt ants in the surrounding grasslands. Warblers are common, buzzards wheel and cry 'cat like' overhead and are now joined by red kites. Ravens have reclaimed these woods and their deep base 'cronk' is a common sound.

The scrub above the woods is biodiversity rich with warblers such as blackcaps and garden warblers hunting the denser patches and redstarts singing from prominent trees. In a few places orchids such as the dark red helleborine are found.

The more sombre conifer woods like those around Ladybower do not have the biodiversity levels of oak or ash woods but they do contain a unique blend of charismatic birds. Goshawks still breed after years of persecution. Crossbills nest annually and siskins have successfully invaded from the north. Ground dwelling plant life can be sparse under the heavy shade of the canopy but fungi populations are strong and attract people in autumn.

Many woods throughout Derbyshire are semi-natural and contain a mixture of native trees with introduced species

A hedgehog rambles through a patch of bluebells seeking out juicy
earthworms and slugs.
A male orange-tip butterfly roosts among the bluebells on a cool day ▶

such as sweet chestnut and larch. They are important for wildlife. Some oak woods support good colonies of purple hairstreak butterflies. The white hairstreak is even more important because its caterpillar's food plant is elm and the vast majority of these died out during the Dutch elm disease outbreak. This highlights that, even with protection, there are factors we are still unable to control that may have an impact on our woods and trees. Acute oak decline is caused by a bacteria that can kill an oak in a couple of years. It is a new disease centred in the English Midlands which has raised real fears for Derbyshire's oaks.

Trees are significant land features. Of particular importance are veteran trees, individuals of great age such as the oaks and alders at Chatsworth, Calke and Kedleston. The Great Trees of Derbyshire project recorded more than 4000 veteran trees with Britain holding a significant proportion of Europe's veterans. These not only provide a living link to our past but as they age they become increasingly wildlife-rich. It seems odd but one of their strategies is to become hollow and short where the top has often snapped off. This reduction in height and weight dramatically decreases their chances of being blown over. The nooks and crannies become important bat roosts and hibernation sites alongside nesting places for barn owls and jackdaws, as well as food for wood-boring beetles and fungi, like the nationally rare oak polypore.

Bank voles are small mammals that forage on the woodland floor. Being vegetarians they eat a wide range of seeds, fruits and green plant material. They are also one of the primary items that feature on the diet sheets of tawny owls!

As summer ends and the chill of autumn sets in many fungi reproduce and appear
as toadstools. Fungi are essential because they break down the dead vegetation
and recycle the nutrients for the next generation of trees. Our interest in fungi
has exploded over the last few decades and many of us now spend time on fungi
forays in the woods in September and October.

Derbyshire Custodians. Irene Brierton, wildlife artist

I love your work and have always wondered where you get your inspiration? I was born in Derbyshire but spent time in Buckinghamshire as a child. On my return I was entranced by the Cromford Canal and its wildlife. Inspiration for my painting is drawn directly from my contact with wildlife which began in childhood.

How did you get involved with badgers? My first encounter with Brock was on a badger watch in Somerset. I was with Simon King and the BBC were filming the event. It was a magical experience and I was hooked. I then joined my local badger group, becoming Chair of the newly formed Mid Derbyshire group in 1990.

You say that you work with the local badger group. What exactly does that entail? It is a very varied job. I answer calls requesting advice, often relating to badgers visiting gardens, as well as responding to calls about casualty badgers. Development issues keep us busy providing advice with regard to the legislation protecting badgers and their setts, which often involves site visits. Badgers can get into some real scrapes and we are called to their rescue. A considerable amount of my time is spent looking into the issue of bovine TB.

You mentioned rescue work. Can you give any examples? One of the oddest was the time we were called out to an abandoned mine shaft. Lying at the bottom were two badgers. Unfortunately one was dead but the other one was still alive. It was quite a struggle to get the live one out from the confined space. Once rescued the badger is checked over by a vet and will receive any necessary treatment. That one was OK. It ate well, slept and was released a couple of nights later. Some are kept longer until fit enough to be returned to the wild. A permanent cover was put on the mine shaft. Another incident involved the rescue of a cub after torrential rain had flooded a sett completely. Its mother was seen washed down river as she valiantly tried to rescue her cubs. She had brought one to safety, which was found, survived and was eventually returned to the wild.

Bovine TB never seems far from the news. How is your work linked to this? We consider the impending cull to be ill advised and wholly unnecessary. I have attended numerous seminars and lectures, many given by eminent scientists in this field, and read a huge amount. A five year study, the Randomised Badger Culling Trail, part of which took place in Derbyshire, concluded that a cull could make no meaningful contribution to the control of bovine TB in cattle. I try wherever possible to put the arguments into perspective and have often been asked to comment on both radio and TV. The postbag on badger culling, following a period of raising public awareness and in response to a Government consultation on the issue, was apparently the largest ever received on a single issue in the UK, with 96% of respondents opposed to the idea - that speaks volumes!

What are your favourite wildlife encounters? There are so many, but I have spent hours at night watching badgers and whilst doing so have had many memorable wildlife encounters. On one occasion a hare appeared around a bend in the wall I was leaning against and we just sat looking at one another - that was amazing. I have introduced others to badger watching and it's lovely to share in their delight at the experience.

Badgers are common in many woodlands, coming out at night to root amongst the soft soil for earthworms, their favourite food.

Tawny and long-eared owls can share the same woods. Tawny owls are very common across Derbyshire and set up their territory in the autumn when their familiar hoots and screeches can be heard.

Long-eared owls are scarcer and much quieter ▶
Like tawnys they often breed very early in the year but instead of normally using holes in trees they prefer an old wood pigeon, crow or sparrowhawk's nest. The chicks of both owls leave the nest before they are feathered and are sometimes thought to be abandoned. Usually they are not and are best left alone for their parents to feed them.

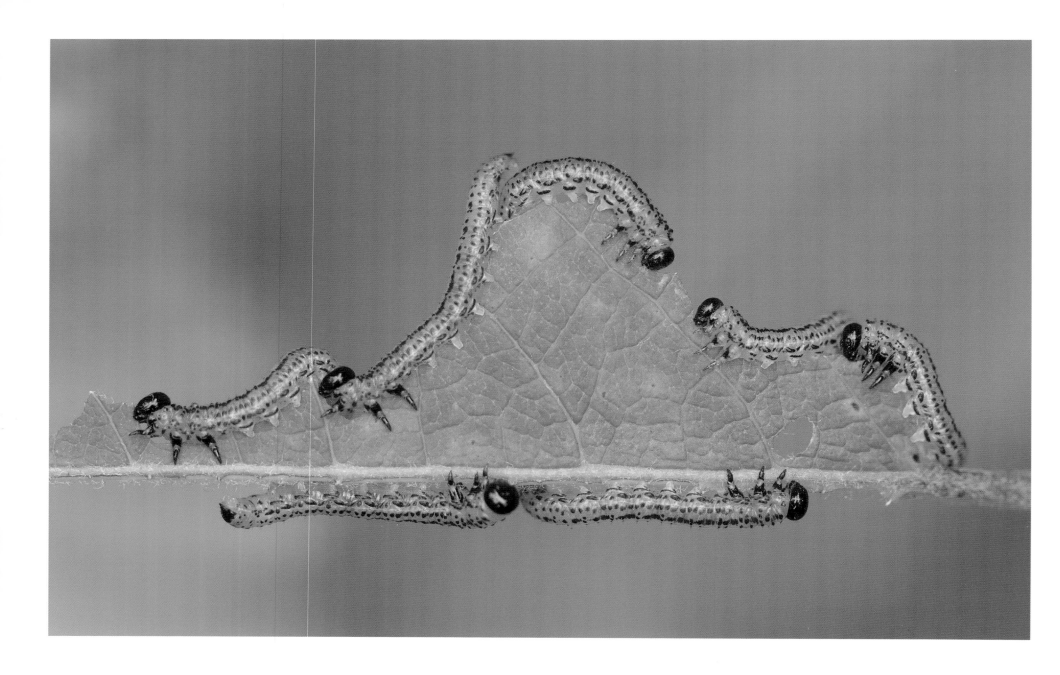

Not all caterpillars belong to moths and butterflies. Many flies, like these birch sawflies, also have caterpillars as their larvae. Birches are more common in the upland parts of Derbyshire, particularly if the soil is acidic. If gamekeepers stopped burning the moors and all the sheep were removed the moorlands would rapidly be colonised by birches and the heather moor would slowly turn back to woodland.

Puss moth caterpillar, burnished brass and 2 buff-tip moths hiding on a birch twig.

Moths and their caterpillars are one of the mainstays in the diet of many woodland birds in the breeding season. Many birds time the laying of their eggs to coincide with the maximum number of caterpillars to give the chicks the best possible chance of survival.

Woodland birds are often heard before seen. Song is important because it's difficult to spot each other, particularly in spring and summer when the canopy is dense. Nuthatches and blue tits are typical small woodland birds with distinctive songs which can be easily found in a variety of woodland such as the extensive ash woods of the Wye Valley or the oak woods around Ladybower.

Woodcock are one of Derbyshire's most secretive birds. They prefer very quiet woods to breed in and are nocturnal. The best time to watch them is at dusk when the males fly in a crude circle, called roding. The woods in the Goyt Valley are one of their favourite places.

Derbyshire Custodians. Emma Barnes, forest manager

Your job title sounds fascinating. Tell me how you became a forest manager? I did a degree in Environmental Science and managed to get a job working for a forestry consultant. I found this too office based and missed the outdoors - getting my hands dirty and creating forests, so my husband and I left our jobs and set up our own company called Native Forestry. We do a range of work but the main thing is that we get to plant all the woodlands we design.

You call your company Native Forestry. Why did you decide on this name? This is very important to us. We have strong beliefs in how woodland should be planted and are very keen to use native species such as oak or birch. We know that many woodland schemes often include 'exotics', possibly because they may be more colourful but their wildlife value is never as high as native species. Take for example the English oak. Up to 300 different invertebrates may live on one tree. This means lots of biodiversity and food for birds and bats. You could choose turkey oak. It looks similar but has far less invertebrates using it, therefore its wildlife value is much lower.

Because of our ecological backgrounds we are fascinated with the whole woodland ecosystem and how it functions. Native species evolved to work in harmony with the physical environment in Britain and this belief drives us forward.

Planting woodlands sounds a fairly simple thing to do but I guess there is much more to it. Yes, that's certainly true. Every situation is different - the soil, water table and exposure all help to determine what species grow well. We need to be able to read these environmental signs when we choose which species of native tree and shrub to plant. The job does not finish with the design, we help with grant applications as well. We plant all the trees ourselves and provide on-going maintenance like scrub clearance, strimming and spot-weed killing to give the young trees every chance of success.

Where in Derbyshire do you do most of your work? We work closely with landowners and often the National Forest so much of our work is in the south of the county and in neighbouring counties like Leicestershire. One of our favourite projects was the creation of a small wood called Short Heath Wood. This is a small community woodland in the National Forest and because of its location the local community uses the woodland a lot which gives us great satisfaction. This wood also joins together some other woodlands so creates corridors for wildlife to move around.

What are your personal wildlife highlights so far? I guess I can answer in two ways. I am fascinated by bats and belong to South Derbyshire Bat Group and I do a lot of bat recording. Bats are amazing animals. At first they don't seem accessible - small, often dark with a rapid flight and only coming out at night, but with a bat detector they are very easy to find and even watch. My other highlight is something that I do very often, spend an hour or two in ancient woodland. It's so magical. The lovely greens with varying shades of brown are beautiful and always create a feeling of calm and peace. It is never dull, whatever the weather or season. Ancient woods are delicate yet large and enduring. I often think they are much understated.

Many Derbyshire woods are carpeted by the stunning azure haze of bluebells in early May. Calke Park and Shaw Wood are two excellent places to chill out and let the colours wash over you.

An orb spider waits patiently amongst a forest of fruiting lichens on the
branch of a birch tree.
Lords and Ladies appear in early spring. Later in the year the pillar-box red
spikes of berries light up the woodland floor. Linacre Woods ▶

Sparrowhawks suffered greatly in the 1970's when a mixture of very toxic pesticides was used on many of our crops. At the top of a short food chain they were hit really hard and numbers plummeted to the point that they became very rare. Eventually the pesticides were banned and sparrowhawk numbers steadily rose. Today they are widespread throughout all of Derbyshire's woodlands.

Goshawks became extinct in Britain due to the attentions of the Victorian gamekeeper. Luckily a group of falconers wanted to see this magnificent bird back in the wild and deliberately released a number into Derbyshire's Dark Peak. The first recorded breeding took place in 1966 and breeding pairs reached double figures by the mid 1980's. The population in Derbyshire is split into two areas but the one in the northern half of the county, which favours conifers on the moorland fringe, is not as successful as the population further south due to persecution.

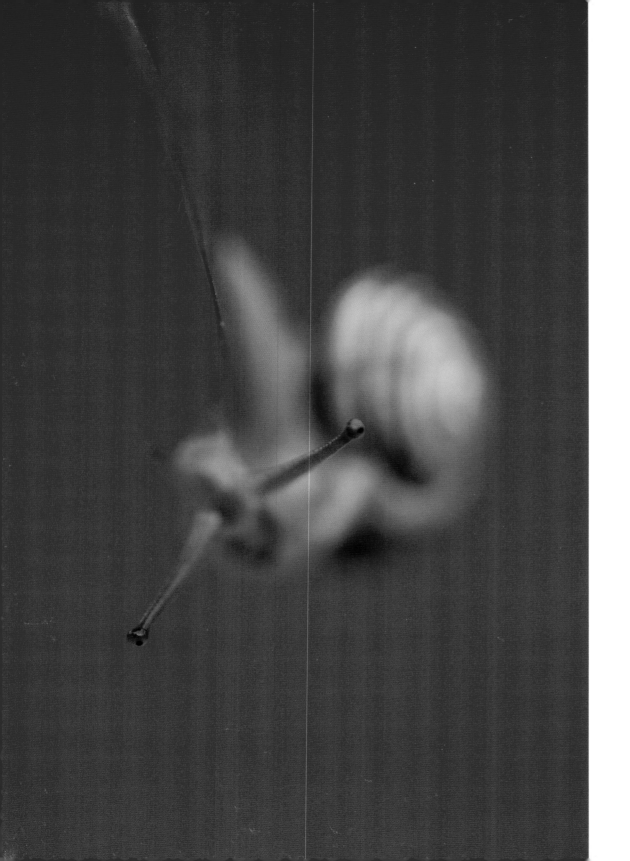

Dormice were recorded in Derbyshire up to 1905 but after that no evidence that they were present has been found. The two great nut hunts of 1993 and 2002, designed to find evidence of this gorgeous, golden mammal, drew a blank for the county. A reintroduction project run by the People's Trust for Endangered Species and Natural England released dormice into the Staffordshire part of the Peak in 2002, the Mid-Derwent Valley in 2003 and the Chatsworth Estate in 2005. Constant monitoring has shown that the Mid-Derwent population did breed initially but seems to have died out. However, the Chatsworth and Staffordshire populations are still present. Dormice are one of the few mammals in Britain that actually hibernate and nest boxes are put up for breeding and hibernating. They prefer coppiced woodland with hazel and honeysuckle so part of any introduction requires good woodland management ▶

Banded snails have great variety in their shell patterns.

The black-dashed, sky-blue wing panel of a jay is possibly one of the most beautiful patterns in the natural world. Jays are getting bolder as persecution reduces. They are incredibly intelligent birds with amazingly sharp eyesight. In autumn they are prodigious acorn hoarders but, unlike grey squirrels who nip out the growing part of the acorn, any nuts forgotten by jays may become the mighty oaks of tomorrow's woodlands.

Derbyshire's Moorlands

Purple as far as the eye can see the heady, delightful cologne of heather honey drifts on the warm August air as a red grouse proudly proclaims his territory. Grouse heads duck down as a raven leisurely floats by whilst a stonechat 'chacks' his displeasure. Derbyshire's moorlands are one of the real gems in the county's landscape and wildlife locker.

The moors in Derbyshire are most extensive in the northern Dark Peak but other strategically important areas exist near Buxton and in the south on the Staffordshire border. The northern moors between Sheffield and Glossop, with the imposing presence of Kinder Scout, are some of the finest uplands in Britain. The famous Snake Pass road, probably the most closed English road due to snow, wends its beautiful way over the Pennines. Further north the M62 takes the brunt of the traffic between east and west.

Kinder Scout, at 636 metres, is the highest point in the Peak and Derbyshire. It is famous not only for its brooding presence, highly changeable weather and incredible landscape but is also a site of some historical importance. Here in 1932 occurred the first mass trespass, a brave and astounding event that changed access to the land and to the Peak from which we all benefit today. North from Kinder runs the vast moorland of Bleaklow with its eroded peat landscape, atmosphere of isolation and mysterious plane wrecks. Wildlife up here is special, if a little sparse. Ravens patrol the air and the ever present mountain hare adds that special feeling of an arctic wilderness.

Derbyshire's moorlands can be divided into 3 types depending on their primary vegetation. The first is typical heather moor where common heather sweeps away to the horizon. Purple in late August, this must rate as one of the great flora experiences anywhere on Earth. Heather does not like it too wet and where the peat starts to deepen and become damper the second vegetation type takes over, cotton grass moor. The nodding, fluffy, white heads in summer bring this damper moor to life. Golden plover, dunlin and curlew all add their incredible songs in spring.

The third main vegetation type is bilberry moor. Not as extensive as the other two and often competing with heather, the red flowers and later delicious, satin skinned berries are important for wildlife. The increasingly rare bilberry bumble bee lives here alongside common lizards.

In low lying places or areas of poor drainage and heavy rain blanket bogs, dominated by sphagnum mosses, will occur. Blanket bog is an internationally rare habitat and Derbyshire has some very fine examples. In summer bog asphodel's lovely yellow flowers nod in the breeze while sundews trap unwary flies.

Moorland may at times seem vast and hardy. Its extreme exposure at the hands of wind, rain and frost gives it a feeling of toughness yet this is far from the truth. Moorland is a farmed and heavily managed habitat that has suffered a lot in the last 100 years. Sheep numbers had risen towards unsustainable levels but, thankfully, have fallen more

◀ As winter turns to summer the mountain hare's fur changes from white to a grey-brown.

Burbage moor.

recently as we have seen the error of overstocking. We are still feeling the effect of too many sheep on the moor and the increase in bracken at the expense of heather is also a serious issue.

Erosion from the millions of trampling feet cause footpaths to widen and where the peat becomes exposed due to loss of vegetation the wind and rain can lower thousands of years of peat accumulation in decades.

The past industrial revolution blackened the faces of our cities and the toxic fumes often blew across the moors raining down their acids onto the fragile mosses and lichens. Hopefully, this legacy of our past has receded with smokeless zones and catalytic converters taking one of main causes of acid rain out of the millions of car exhausts.

Dry, hot summers bring their own problems and fires that start from a camp barbeque can burn deep and remove the protective covering of heather. The moor is deliberately burnt on a rotational system and many reported fires are really these controlled burns. To the uninitiated this may seem madness but as long as it is done before the nesting season and in a controlled manner it is really a vital part of moorland management. Strips of burn allow the heather to regenerate providing the grouse with fresh food and in the older, deeper heather secret places to nest undisturbed.

Shooting occurs on many of the county's moors and, whilst this may evoke a mixed response, it does bring much needed cash into the local economy and keeps the moors vibrant and fresh. Controlled heather burns benefit other forms of wildlife by providing a mixed mosaic of heather ages. If moorland is left completely undisturbed in the absence of sheep it would slowly revert back to woodland, initially with the very fertile birch and eventually back to oak. This may not seem such a bad thing but we would lose some of the county's best wildlife hotspots and landscapes.

Moorland management is a complex and expensive enterprise and in many cases groups of like minded organisations are pooling their expertise and resources to bring the moors back to their former glory. The National Trust and RSPB now work together to manage the vast and superb Eastern Moors. Moors for the Future, a consortia of Natural England, the National Trust, RSPB, Peak National Park, Yorkshire Water, Severn Trent Water, Derbyshire County Council and United Utilities have successfully been granted millions of pounds from the Lottery to restore areas of damaged moorland.

One of their more recent and exciting initiatives is the Moorlife Protecting Active Blanket Bogs scheme. Experimental fencing on Kinder Scout by the National Trust has shown that vegetation restoration is possible when sheep numbers are reduced and heather seed, collected locally, is added to the barren, eroding peats. This technique has now been extended to Bleaklow. Drainage channels have been blocked in an attempt to increase the wetness of the tops and to help stimulate the growth of the fabulous sphagnum moss and cotton grass.

Many of Derbyshire's moorlands carry international protection because of the stunning array of superb breeding birds such as merlins and short-eared owls.

Many of Derbyshire's moors carry the highest levels of conservation status for good reasons. These moors are incredible places for wildlife. Often birds grab the headlines because they tend to be more obvious and there is a long tradition of bird watching in the UK. Here peregrines swoop in tremendous power dives on unsuspecting woodpigeons whilst the plucky, diminutive merlin hunts low over the heather seeking out meadow pipits. Ravens returned to breed in 1992 but there is still cause for concern. The Peak's moors should have at least a handful of regular nesting hen harriers yet we have none!

Black grouse are back following a reintroduction programme in the late 1990's. Whinchats seem to have almost disappeared but stonechat numbers are rising. Wheatears are still around though they can be more easily watched in the White Peak. Adders occur in a few places on East moor but are not commonly distributed across the extensive uplands. In spring, on south facing bilberry patches green hairstreaks challenge your eye to follow them and later the large and stunning emperor moth can be found resting amongst the bilberry.

Moorland wildlife is special though not always easy to find in the vastness of heather or bilberry. It is also vulnerable and accordingly many moors have varied levels of legal protection. These range from European designations like Special Protection Areas to UK designations such as Sites of Special Scientific Interest. On top of these there are now many far-reaching schemes like the RSPB's Futurescapes and Natural England's Nature Improvement Areas, both having examples within the Dark Peak's moorlands.

Common (or viviparous) lizards are widespread across many of Derbyshire's
moors. They are even found sunbathing on the top of the Snake Pass.
Derbyshire's adders feed on them as do many birds, including ring ouzels.
These super little reptiles come in a variety of colour forms. This male is the
most common type, being a subtle medley of browns. However, green or
even bluish ones are also found on our moors.
The lizards feed on a variety of small insects such as these shiny black ants
that are exploring their mossy world as the sun shines through a series of
water droplets after a light shower ▶

Odin's bird, the raven, now regularly patrols many of the gritstone edges on the lookout for an easy meal. The deep basal 'cronk' is one good indicator they are around as is the tumbling flight as they play with the gusts and eddies that sweep up from the valleys below. Derwent Edge and Salt Cellar ▶

Green hairstreaks are early butterflies usually found on the wing in May. They love south-facing moorland slopes that are thick with bilberries. When they rest they blend in so well with the vibrant greens of the leaves that they are virtually impossible to spot. They are found on many moors throughout Derbyshire from the Roaches to Derwent Edge and the slopes of Kinder in the north.

The emperor is a large and showy moth flying in May and June. The female is larger because she has to produce eggs. The caterpillars feed on heather and are green with tufts of black bristles.

Derbyshire Custodians. Roger France, gamekeeper, Snake Moors.

I am going to guess that your year is dictated entirely by red grouse. Is that true?

Yes, though the seasons play a part as well. In winter we burn the heather in a controlled way when there are no nesting birds. Without this there would be no golden plover, grouse or curlews as the whole moor would slowly turn back to woodland. I also control some of the predators now like stoats, foxes and crows. As spring starts I look for crow's nests and try to keep their numbers down to reduce predation of grouse eggs and chicks. In summer I count grouse and repair paths and shooting butts. In August and September the shooting season is underway and I help with advice and organising the beaters.

I have noticed in some years that grouse numbers are much higher than others. Why is this?

The theory is that a parasite of the grouse, the strongylosis worm, builds up and weakens the birds, which ultimately fall in numbers. It is when the grouse population is low and weaker that predators like crows can have a major impact. The parasite seems to go in cycles so we get a few good years, like the last three, followed by years with far less grouse.

I sometimes hear criticisms of gamekeepers and their work. How would you argue against this?

I find that by explaining the workings of the moor and how we maintain it by burning heather and controlling predators most people understand and it allays their fears. Bad publicity about the perceived persecution of birds of prey never helps. I would be lying to say it never happens but it is rare today and old prejudices seem to take a long time to die. In terms of my area the number of buzzards, peregrines, sparrowhawks and ravens has risen dramatically in the last few years. I see kites occasionally and even ospreys. Merlins are always about though the number of goshawks is not high but they are breeding in a few woods around the area. For things to improve I believe that a more enlightened attitude and air of cooperation is needed by all sides, especially if we want to see hen harriers breeding regularly.

How has the wildlife changed in your area during your time here as a gamekeeper?

I have been one of the keepers on the Snake Moors from 1968 to 2010 so I have seen a lot of changes. Black grouse have gone, bar the few that have been reintroduced. Birds of prey have rocketed. As a young lad I never thought I would ever see a peregrine, now I see them most days when I am out. Lapwings have tumbled, red squirrels gone, though that occurred fairly recently. I even remember seeing an almost black one with gorgeous ear tufts. Badger numbers are now very high, foxes stable and ring ouzels and skylarks have dropped dramatically.

What are your favourite wildlife experiences?

I love red grouse but to see a black grouse in flight is superb. Bigger than the red but much faster. I have killed a lot of foxes but I really admire them as animals, they are so intelligent. I always feel sad when I have to kill one.

Golden plovers return to the moors in the spring having spent the winter at a lower elevation, often on farm land or marshes. Their haunting, mournful call is so in keeping with the wild, wind-swept, open expanses of Derbyshire's moorlands. Possibly the easiest place to watch or listen to them is from the paved Pennine Way footpath as it cuts across the peat and cotton grass on the Snake summit.

Red grouse dominate the heather moors in the north of Derbyshire. As game they are shot in good breeding years and the wildlife and landscape of the moor is inextricably linked to these charismatic birds. They are present all year round, even in the hardest of winters. They usually feed on moorland plants such as heather and bilberry but in extreme winters like those of 2010 I watched a few grouse perched high up in a bush feeding on hawthorn berries.

The chicks hatch in late May and are gorgeous fluffy bundles already possessing distinctive personalities. Wet weather during their first few weeks is probably their biggest threat.

Coach and Horses, Derwent Edge.

Bumblebees have an important role to play in the ecology of moorlands. This queen bilberry bumblebee fertilises the early flowers of a bilberry plant ensuring that the small, satin-black, vitamin C-rich berries will be present in late summer and provide an autumn feast for many animals.

Where water collects bogs can form. These are nutrient poor and some plants have devised alternative strategies to get their protein-forming nitrates. Derbyshire's moors do have a select few carnivorous plants like this sundew. The sticky filament ends trap and digest unwary insects.

Derbyshire Custodians. Kath Birkinshaw, tenant hill farmer.

Your year must be firmly dictated by the weather?

In the late autumn we gather the ewes and put them to the rams on the hay fields then they are moved to the rougher pastures on the farm where we feed them over the winter. During the winter the short days are dominated with feeding the stock. If we can find any spare time we repair the dry stone walls around the farm and add last year's muck to the hay meadows. Lambing occurs later on hill farms in April because of the harsh weather. This is probably the busiest time of the year and we hardly ever get a full night's sleep. The sheep are on the hay meadows until the 10th of May when they are then moved to the rougher pastures. The hay meadows can then flower and, if we are lucky, we may get our hay cut in late July after the wild flowers have set seed, though in the last few years we haven't managed to get the hay in until September. Then it's back to our own sheep plus some contract shepherding for other farmers.

How traditional is hill farming today?

My farm is owned by the National Trust so a lot of my management is geared towards a wildlife-rich and traditional method of farming. We do a lot by hand and try to reduce chemical use where possible. When we control weeds like thistles we either scythe them by hand or, with the help of my sister, add weed killer to each individual thistle. We often turn the hay by hand, still using the old, yet very efficient, wooden hay rakes and we produce square bales. Muck is still the main way of adding nutrients to help the hay grow.

You mentioned the hay meadows. Are these wild flower rich?

Our hay meadows are very important. They have a really high biodiversity and we farm them for both a hay crop and to get the best from the wild flowers. We are having a problem at the moment with yellow rattle, normally a desirable wild flower, which is now taking over the fields. Yellow rattle is a parasitic flower on grasses and we have so much that the hay crop is now really small and not enough to feed the stock over winter. In the past lime was added to the meadows and this seemed to keep the yellow rattle down a bit allowing the wild grasses and other flowers to do well. We are going to try liming again to see if it helps.

You're very passionate about your job. What aspects appeal the most?

I love working with animals and being outdoors. I feel it's in my bones to be a hill farmer and shepherd. My sister works the farm with me and we make a great team. The best aspect is probably the changing seasons - the coming of spring and longer days after winter, the first birds returning to the farm like the ring ouzel that visits the hay meadows, and swallows around the barns. It's a tough lifestyle but one I would never change.

A small heath butterfly roosting on a rainy day on a harebell. Small heaths are probably the most abundant moorland butterfly in Derbyshire.

A huge moorland sky ominously presses down on a lonely, wind battered birch straddling the Sheffield-Derbyshire border.

Moss sporangia, Longdendale. Mosses do not set seed but produce
spores in sporangia, a bit like the seed heads of flowering plants.

The hen harrier, alongside the goshawk, is the bird that suffers the most persecution in Derbyshire. We should have a thriving population of these charismatic birds breeding on our moors but their habit of taking grouse brings them directly into conflict with shooting interests. In years past they bred on many of Derbyshire's grouse moors. Alas, the effectiveness of the Victorian gamekeeper banished them to the history books, or so it looked until 1987 when a pair appeared in the Goyt Valley.

A successful watch was placed on the nest and the pair raised chicks to fledging. Was this the beginning of better days for the hen harrier? Unfortunately the answer was no.

The birds failed to breed the following year in the Goyt Valley and it was not until 2006 when two females laid five eggs each in two nests only a couple of kilometres apart in the Upper Derwent Valley that the story takes on a positive note again. Only one male was ever seen and he disappeared soon after egg laying. A watch was placed on both nests and the decision to artificially feed both females to help them raise their chicks was taken. This proved an amazing success and all ten eggs hatched and all the chicks fledged.

Hopes were high that the following year would see more hen harriers breeding but though some birds did appear and in 2008 tried to nest again it seems that the hen harrier no longer breeds in Derbyshire. The ways and means to help rare birds are well known but in the case of the hen harrier they clearly fail. It is easy to apportion blame but perhaps we need to take a fresh, more enlightened look at how we reconcile grouse and shooting interests and the success of moorland raptors.

Male ring ouzel, Seal Moor.

Once a common game bird across the whole of Britain, black grouse became extinct in Derbyshire in 1992. A couple of centuries before they were described as more common than red grouse! The black grouse project aims to get this incredible bird back into the county. The upper Derwent Valley was chosen as the initial release site because it contains the mosaic of habitats needed. The project was to run for six years with thirty birds a year being released from 2003. After three years the release site was moved further east towards the Strines area. Black grouse are definitely back in Derbyshire and have certainly bred in the Strines area. The population seems to be mobile with leking males on some of the moors around the upper Derwent Valley.

Derbyshire Custodians. Simon Wright, the National Trust's countryside manager for the Dark Peak and Longshaw.

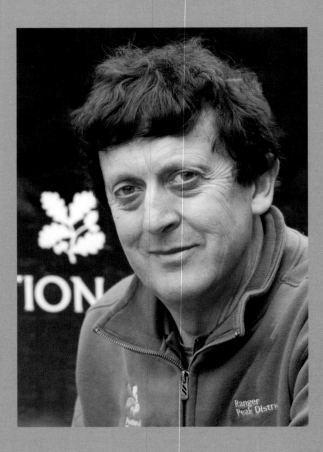

What's your team working on at the moment?
A great deal but I suppose the most interesting is the work on moorland restoration, particularly on Kinder Scout and Bleaklow. Alongside our Projects team and contractors we are currently fencing Kinder Scout plateau to remove the pressure of grazing sheep on new vegetation, building on similar work on Bleaklow. This is multi agency work, some under the umbrella of the Moors for the Future Partnership. We are also re-wetting the tops by blocking natural drainage gullies, to encourage the peat bogs to reform and reduce peat loss. Nearly all of our land is farmed by tenants and we want them to be part of our vision for a wildlife rich and sustainable living moorland, benefiting vulnerable species such as golden plover and sphagnum moss.

Which aspects of your work give you most satisfaction?
I really enjoy working for the National Trust because our protection is permanent, once designated our land can never be sold without the involvement of Parliament. This means that we can manage for the future, with a long term vision. A lot of what we do now will benefit people and wildlife for generations to come. I love the idea that I have had a hand in that and you can see changes already. I enjoy working with my team and meeting the public. Contact with our visitors and passing our message on to others is a really satisfying part of my work.

Countryside Manager is a wide ranging description, so what does your job actually entail?
I manage the 'open spaces team' for the National Trust. In a sense they are the front line troops that carry out or oversee vital conservation work and liaise with the public and our partners. They have an in-depth knowledge of their patch, with a good feeling for local relationships and communities.

Which aspect of the Dark Peak's wildlife gives you the biggest buzz?
That's an easy one - the changing colour of the mountain hares through the seasons, the first calls of golden plover as they arrive back on the moors in spring and swathes of white cotton grass heads on the moorland in early summer.

Derbyshire's mountain hares are animals of the arctic, turning white in winter to avoid predators. Unfortunately because of the lack of snow in many winters it may actually be a disadvantage. They should not really be here, it is too far south, but the Victorians introduced them into Derbyshire from Scotland so they could hunt them. The hares survived and today add that splash of arctic wildlife to moorland walks.

Adders are not common in Derbyshire and are mainly confined to an extended colony on Big Moor and East Moor. A few individuals emerge as early as February to bask in the winter sunshine. By April virtually all have left hibernation and are either seeking a mate or looking for food. Adders are the world's most northerly snake and are designed to live in harsh, cold climates. One adaptation is to give birth to young snakes instead of laying eggs. Youngsters are born in August. Adult males can be a striking silver and black, though many look like the browner females.

A number of the acidic pools that are scattered across many moorlands have healthy populations of dragon and damselflies. The diminutive, yet stunningly marked, black darter is a late emerging species that can occur in its hundreds at a few sites.

Unlike Scotland, there are few herds of red deer roaming the moors and until fairly recently there were very few red deer living wild in Derbyshire. Today there are at least two herds of wild reds, one in the Goyt Valley, the other on Big Moor. This latter herd has increased dramatically and is now spreading over a wider area. Both herds almost certainly started with escapees from some of the deer parks like Lyme Park and Chatsworth. Silhouetted against the evening sky, an adult male red is an impressive sight. However, as numbers increase they will start to come into conflict with the management of many moors as their grazing pressure intensifies on the fragile, slow growing plant life. Road accidents will almost certainly increase and culling may have to be introduced to control their numbers.

71

Derbyshire's Farmland

Farming, like many other industries in the UK, has undergone massive changes in the last sixty years. The end of World War II saw great pressures exerted on farmers to maximise production - we didn't want to experience rationing again! Pesticides and fertilisers started to rain down on the soil and many old farming practices such as crop rotation, traditional hay meadows and mixed farming declined. Hedges were grubbed out and new crops appeared.

Farmland is not natural. It is a landscape created by humans that can be wildlife-rich whilst we maintain its primary aim, that of producing food that is healthy and affordable. Luckily Derbyshire farming was not affected with the extreme changes that occured elsewhere in Britain. During the last couple of decades we have started to wake up to agri-environmental issues. Schemes to reduce over-production or to boost farm wildlife came and went. Some like the Environmentally Sensitive Area schemes were very positive. Others such as Set-aside had minimal impact on wildlife.

Today we are far more enlightened with progressive environmental schemes like Countryside Stewardship helping farmers to regain their status as custodians of the countryside. Many organisations now play advisory roles, for example the RSPB with its lapwing and twite friendly farming advice and the Wildlife Trusts with their progressive Living Landscapes initiatives.

Farmers in Derbyshire face a new future. We now realise the land is not solely about producing food. It is our countryside and we want to watch the wildlife in it, or at least know that wildlife is there, thriving and being catered for. Over the next few decades we should hopefully see new hedges planted, wild flower meadows protected, farm birds rise in number and wetlands, dew ponds and flood meadows managed for wildlife.

Farming has another effect on our lives, it is the essence of what many of us think of as the countryside. It has an incredibly important aesthetic appeal and Derbyshire farming is on the whole very attractive. Most of Derbyshire is a land of small farms, many run by a single person or family. Small fields dotted with sheep or black and white Friesian cows separated by stone walls produces a beautiful landscape.

Dairy and beef farming, particularly across a lot of the limestone plateau and in the valleys between the moors, is typical of Derbyshire but are under threat. Milk quotas and very low milk prices have caused a dramatic decline in dairy farming. The number of dairy farms in Derbyshire has plummeted from 842 to 460 between 1996 and 2007. The danger here is that as farmers lose their dairy herds they diversify into something else, perhaps horse stables or craft shops. Some farms are bought to convert to other uses or by hobby farmers and we may be in danger of losing the character of the land.

◄ Farming on the limestone plateau near Litton.

Wildflower meadows declined dramatically after the second world war. Today we view them in a different light and parts of many farmland conservation schemes aim to protect, enhance or even recreate these visual feasts.

It could be argued that virtually all of Derbyshire is farmland. The moors to the north are managed for sheep. Here dry stone walls of gritstone are an integral part of Derbyshire's farming landscape as are the limestone walls to the south. Over the past few decades fields have been slowly enlarged to accommodate bigger machinery but in a few places the older, long, thin stone-walled fields can still be found.

Farmland can be rich in wildlife and Derbyshire's is particularly so, primarily because many of the farms remain small and are less intensively managed. Brown hares can be watched boxing in March as the clatter of wings of a male pheasant breaks the dawn air. Grey partridges wander along hedgerow bottoms and the black and white wings of lapwings cleave the air. Hedges provide shelter and highways across the open fields and allow small mammals such as wood mice and bank voles to skitter about, hopefully without drawing the attention of a buzzard above.

In winter thrushes from Scandinavia feed in the damp earth or when the cold weather locks this larder shut they switch to the hawthorn berries on the hedges. Farm wildlife watching can be very rewarding and areas around Carsington or Kedleston retain the ancient feel of old farming, pleasing to the eye and rich in character and wildlife.

New crops come and go as fashion and agriscience change. Today we can see the 'New York taxi cab' yellow of swathes of oil seed rape blazing across the countryside. As our energy resources dwindle we are starting to look to biofuels. Perhaps we will see more fields of willow, a potentially excellent wildlife resource as well as an ideal wood for furnaces.

Farming is an ever changing industry but with our more enlightened views today and the advice and protection of the Peak Park and others hopefully we can see farmland regain its former wildlife riches and still provide a solid rural economy together with the stunning scenery that we all cherish.

Wood pigeon. A successful farmland bird that is now spreading into our urban spaces.

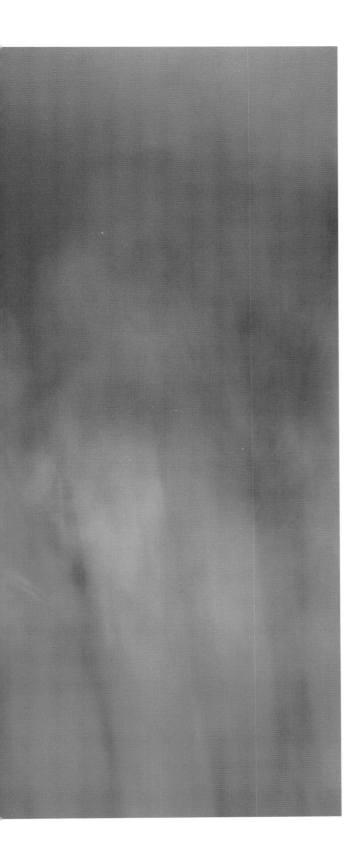

It would be a bit cheeky to say that rabbits are everyone's friend though many of us do find them cute. In the 1930's it was estimated that rabbits ate roughly one third of all vegetables grown in the UK. Myxomatosis was seen as the solution and the disease still exists today. Rabbits are not native to Britain. There is some evidence that suggests they were introduced by the Romans though many believe they were introduced a 1000 years later by the Normans. Today they are an integral part of farming and grassland ecology with many animals dependant on them for food and many grassland wildflowers benefiting from their selective grazing.

Winter sees Scandinavian visitors, like the fieldfare above, joining our more familiar blackbirds and song thrushes across a lot of Derbyshire's farmland. Every now and then winter is harder than normal and snow persists for weeks on end. Old orchards and hedges, if laden with berries, are now vital for survival. Where food does occur, hunger - driven desperation and the cold over-rides normal behaviour and fights may break out!

Cowslips are found occasionally in old pastures which have not been ploughed for many years. Fritillaries are found in abundance in one field in the east of Derbyshire. They were probably planted many years ago and have increased ever since and alongside cowslips they make a spectacular display in late April or early May.

Foxes are widespread and abundant throughout Derbyshire. The practice of farming with small fields and hedges suits them admirably. This young adult was photographed at Unstone during a summer project.

The tale of the buzzard over the last 30 years is one of the great success stories in Britain. Buzzards are now arguably the most common bird of prey in our country and are widespread across all of Derbyshire. They prefer the softer, more food-rich, farmland of the south compared to the rougher moors in the north and west of the county. Buzzards are very adaptable feeders and will eat anything from earthworms to dead carcasses. Small fields with hedges dotted here and there, and small woods are the ideal country for this superb raptor. It is true to say that persecution against raptors has declined dramatically since the Victorian era but we need to be ever vigilant because it still does occur today!

Derbyshire Custodians. Mike Deakin, Trent Valley farmer.

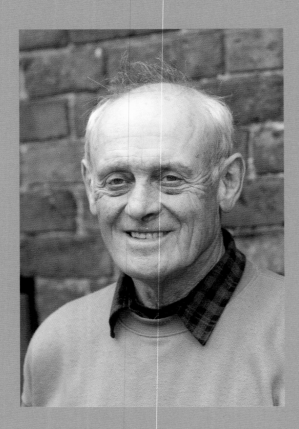

Mike, how has your farm changed over the last few decades?
There have been many changes, probably the biggest was deciding to lose our dairy herd seven years ago and concentrate on arable farming and farming for wildlife. We decided to sell the dairy cattle because milk prices were incredibly low and we wanted to diversify into other areas.

Is your farm a typical one in South Derbyshire?
Yes it is. It's a small family-owned farm of 190 acres. We have decided like many around us to become involved in the National Forest scheme. We now have 65 acres devoted to woodland. The rest is farmed on a rotation using wheat, oil seed rape and forage maize.

Can you describe the National Forest scheme?
The scheme asks farmers to tender a proposal to the National Forest. We were successful in our bid and they paid us three quarters of the grant in the first year and the balance in year six. Alongside this there is a Forestry Commission grant, which runs for 15 years, after which no further payment will be received.

How have you managed these 65 acres?
We have planted most of the area with native trees, 45% oak and a mix of birch with some ash. We have put in a small stand of larch and Scots pine. We decided we would like to recreate wet woodlands so we blocked some drains and planted willow and alder. We have cleared areas for wildflower meadows and created a dragonfly pond.

I can tell that you are incredibly passionate about wildlife. What other things have you done to benefit animals and plants?
We have created field margins around all our fields. Some of these are six metres wide. In these we planted wild flower mixes and now get good displays of plants like cowslips, yarrow, knapweed, musk mallow and field scabious. These attract butterflies and many other insects. We have to mow them occasionally to stop the blackthorn taking over. I also plant one acre per year with plants that produce lots of seeds and leave this every winter for birds to feed on. We now get good flocks of yellow hammers, tree sparrows and reed buntings. It makes a great sight to see these lovely birds in winter. I have put up lots of nest boxes as well. We have even recorded harvest mice, something I am really excited about.

What is your biggest wildlife thrill on your farm?
Without a doubt it is watching the barn owl chicks fledging every year. We never had these in the old days and now we have a pair using one of the nest boxes. Last year they produced a brood of six. We have the pellets analysed and can see what they eat. The dominant food item is the short-tailed field vole. This means that we are getting the field margins right and they can support good populations of these little rodents.

There is no more quintessential farmland bird than the rook. Rooks love the company of humans and many rookeries are close to farms. Rooks have had a chequered past when it comes to farmers. Today we now understand the great benefit they bring when they work the fields looking for wire worms. In 2010 there were in excess of 2200 nests in Derbyshire with their favourite rookery tree being the sycamore.

Mistle thrushes are well known for using nonconventional
materials to build their nests. Here at Unstone one is collecting
pieces of discarded bailer twine from the farmyard.

As autumn approaches sheep's sorrel and dock produce copious amounts of seeds for the coming winter. These seeds are often very dry so bullfinches regularly visit ponds to drink.

Little owls are a fairly recent acquisition to Britain. Originally released by Lord Lilford and others in the mid 1800's they have successfully spread and there are many pairs in Derbyshire. They prefer old pasture fields where there are walls and old trees to nest in.

When we think of farmland birds we often think of starlings. Once so common that we took them for granted we have now realised that their numbers have been reduced greatly over the last 30 years. In good years Kirk Ireton and Middleton Moor have been the place to witness mumurations, the fantastic displays of winter starlings coming in to roost in the evening.

Roe deer numbers are increasing at an amazing rate today. Most are seen at dawn when they leave the sanctuary of the woods to graze in the farmer's fields. Once the diurnal human activity cycle begins with the first cars of the day they retreat back to the shelter of the trees.

Red-legged partridges are an introduced species, sometimes still called by their old name of French partridges. Large numbers are bred to be shot and they are common farmland birds adding a touch of colour to the brown fields and green crops. Unfortunately the native English partridge is not as common.

Female kestrel resting among the bright red poppies of summer.

Wild flower meadow ▶

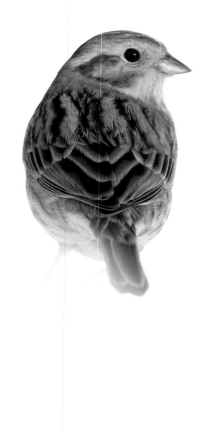

When the snow settles across farmland it creates a magical, quiet world. Whilst this may mean dusting down the sledges for many of us it's a different matter for farmland wildlife. As long as the snow is thin hares can still graze the short grasses and crops that were planted in autumn ▶
For small birds like yellow hammers it may make it very difficult to find the life-saving seeds hidden below the white coat.

The Dales and Grasslands

Small, dry stone walled fields create a unique and special landscape on the 300 metre high Derbyshire limestone plateau. These fields are predominantly used for grazing and grass production. Cutting into the limestone are a number of superb valleys, collectively known as the Derbyshire Dales. The natural vegetation should be ash forest but the continual nibbling of cattle, sheep and rabbits has produced some of the best limestone grasslands in Britain. Here the plant biodiversity is incredibly high with some very special plants including cranesbills, cowslips, hoary plantain, grass-of-Parnassus and various species of orchids. Some of these create the best floral displays anywhere in Britain.

There can be little to rival the spectacular flowering of thousands of early purple orchids on the banks of Cressbrook Dale. Add to this the rich yellows of cowslips, the Exmoor ponies keeping the scrub at bay and the imposing Peter's Stone looking down at you and it is hard to imagine a better backdrop for a break in a walk to drink in the beauty of the view. In late spring dingy skippers cavort low to the ground, perhaps not likely to raise everyone's pulse rate, though the orange - tips visiting the pale pink cuckoo flowers should go some way to compensate. A little later in June Derbyshire's own unique version of the brown argus seeks out the yellow flowered rock-rose to lay its eggs. Hay Dale and Coombes Dale are places to enjoy this special butterfly. Later still many of the dales will see the vigorous, energetic, dark green fritillary. This large and showy butterfly rarely seems to stop, flitting rapidly from one nectar - rich flower to the next.

Earlier in the year brimstones glide amongst the buckhorn, the females distinguished by their pale green wings in contrast to the richer yellows of the male.

Like so much of Derbyshire's landscape, the dales are managed both for agriculture and wildlife. Many of them are protected, some are owned by the National Trust, others managed by Natural England. Grazing is used to keep the hawthorn scrub at bay and the grasslands vibrant with wildflowers.

In the past many areas experienced lead mining and small lead spoil heaps abound. On some of these vernal sandwort prospers because it is tolerant of the toxic heavy metal, earning it its county nickname of 'leadwort'. Priestcliffe Lees is a great area to look for these small white flowers alongside the gorgeous yellow mountain pansy.

Three plants are worthy of a special mention. The first, bird's foot sedge, a rare plant that was first discovered on the valley sides above Water-cum-Jolly. The second is Jacob's ladder, a tall, blue flowered plant that is the county plant of Derbyshire. In recent years this has seen a big increase in numbers and it has spread down the damp valley floor of Lathkill Dale. The third is the enigmatic and arguably the most spectacular British flower, the lady's slipper orchid. Once growing wild near Matlock and in many of the dales this was collected to extinction years ago. An imaginative project headed by the world famous Kew Gardens has seen

◀ Abandoned quarry in Miller's Dale.

Early purple orchids, Cressbrook Dale.

thousands of these gorgeous plants bred and scattered into likely places in its old range and some of these have been planted back into less well visited spots of Derbyshire.

Plant collection was rife during the Victorian times and many parlours had a herbarium or a glass fronted fernery. The steep cliffs on the sides of many dales have superb collections of feathery ferns such as maidenhair spleenwort and brittle bladder fern. Once rare, these are now re-establishing themselves and adding a verdant splash to the grey-white cliff faces.

Each limestone dale has its own specific charm. Some are very pretty and, in consequence, well visited. On any sunny Sunday in summer it is best to avoid the beauty of Dove Dale; leave it until a quiet week day outside of the school holidays! Others, like Lathkill Dale, are very special and have been designated as National Nature Reserves.

Many of the dales have clear, trout rich, bubbling streams running in the valley bottoms, though a number are dry as the stream has retreated underground. Some dales such as Long Dale and Monk's Dale are much quieter, in part because there are no easy car parks and because they have steeper sides creating a darker more secretive atmosphere.

The mossy woods in Monk's Dale have a quiet, fairy-like feel that cannot be found anywhere else in Derbyshire. In Beresford Dale Isaak Walton honed his fly-fishing skills with his young friend Charles Cotton. Bradford Dale near Youlgreave is enriched by its population of dippers and water voles. Monsal Dale and the popular Monsal Head are incredibly impressive and the abandoned railway has been converted into a delightful thirteen kilometre walk. A far more adventurous walk is the Limestone Way, a four or five day hike which wends its way from the south of Castleton, through many of the dales and over the field studded plateau of Derbyshire, to Rocester on the banks of the River Dove.

A slow worm scents the air in spring, Youlgreave.

Redstarts are often considered to be woodland birds and in general that is true in Derbyshire. However, a few pairs nest in cliff faces and old dry stone walls in many of the limestone dales like Lathkill, Coombes and Cressbrook.

The chirping of grasshoppers drifting up from the jungle of sweet grasses is one of the best sounds of summer.

◄ From the air Lathkill Dale is seen to be a wooded valley cut deep into the limestone plateau. The steep sides saved many ash woods from the axe of the early settlers and preserved these fantastic wildlife-rich woodlands for us to enjoy today. Running through the dale is the River Lathkill, dry in the upper part, later becoming a crystal clear river with its own unique variety of brown trout. Extensive lead mining occurred in the valley and this cut through a number of the then separate aquifers. The River Lathkill is an aquifer - filled river and the joining of these is partly responsible for longer lengths of the river becoming dry.

To the horizon stretch dry stone walled fields and in the distance the heather moors of the Dark Peak.

Thorpe Cloud, below, dominates the southern Limestone Dales.

Spotted flycatchers nest in many of the ash woods and, in many dales, often use holes in the low limestone cliffs to build their nests. They are amazing birds to watch and entertain with superb aerial skills when they hawk for flies and other insects.

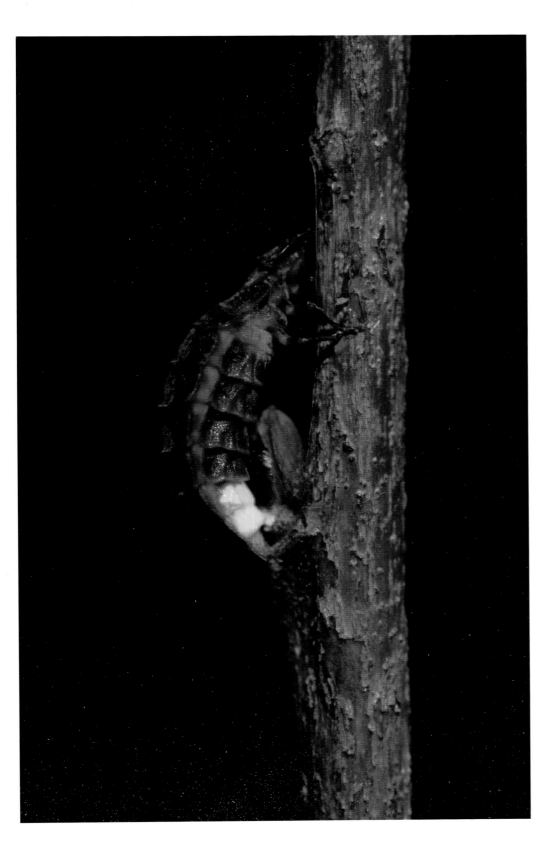

Glow-worms are not really worms at all but predatory beetles that eat snails. They are found in a few of the dales and on an old abandoned railway line near Derby. The last place may seem odd until you realise that the tracks are laid onto limestone ballast. That is the clue. Snails need lots of calcium to form their shells so tend to be more abundant in limestone areas.

I once read a charming story where small boys collected jam jars full of glow-worms to hang in their tents so they could read their comics at night! This sounds credible but when I photographed glow-worms I quickly found that if I touched one by accident it tended to shut down the 'alien' green glow in about three minutes, so I started to think the author was pulling someone's leg!

The queen of the British flora, this is an incredibly elegant and beautiful orchid collected to extinction in Derbyshire and in most of Britain during the great 'orchidelirium' by the Victorians. A single specimen was later discovered in North Yorkshire in 1930 and may be the only true British native lady's slipper. Along with Kew, the world leaders in plant breeding, Natural England has pioneered a tricky reintroduction programme known as the Sainsbury project.

Lady's slippers have proven really difficult to propagate and many of the plants put back into the wild have not survived. The whole project is clouded with secrecy since the great orchid collecting days of the Victorians are definitely not over. Fears are very real that any plants found may be dug up! Some of the reintroductions have taken place in Derbyshire and whilst it is sad that their locations have to be kept secret it's great to know that this stunning flower is now here again.

Common blue resting on bird's-foot trefoil. The common blue butterfly flies throughout the limestone grasslands in the middle to late summer. The males are a dazzling blue whilst the females only have a smudge of blue on their brown upper wings. Both sexes have beautiful markings on their under wings. Bird's-foot trefoil, a common, low growing, yellow flowered grassland plant is the food for their caterpillars.

Common spotted orchids (above) are found growing in a wide variety of places from roadside verges to old quarries. They flower in spring and add an amazing splash of the exotic to many grasslands.

◀ Fly orchid growing in an abandoned limestone quarry near Matlock.

Quarrying in Derbyshire, particularly the Peak National Park, is a controversial issue. New quarries provide income and employment yet are strongly opposed at the planning stage. It is easy to see why but when they cease their working life many become botanical havens and are given nature reserve status. The quarry floor develops soil at a very slow rate which is ideal for many orchids and the rocky faces provide excellent nesting ledges for peregrines and ravens. Once vegetation takes hold they become quiet, peaceful places full of wildlife.

Jacob's ladder, recently voted the county plant of Derbyshire. Lathkill Dale.

Mountain pansies grow in many of the dales. Most are a vibrant butter yellow but it is never hard to find the scarcer purple variety.

Resembling a velvety, fat - bodied bumble bee crowned in green with wings of lilac, bee orchids are well named. The plant's idea is to fool a male bee into mating with it and as it does so one or two sacs of pollen, called pollinia, hopefully stick to it. When the bee is duped by the next flower it should pollinate it. The flowers also have another trick to help attract the unwitting male. Not only do they look like a bee, they actually smell like a female one too - at least to male bees!

Bee orchids are found in a variety of places across Derbyshire. Many are abandoned quarries like those in Miller's Dale, but perhaps the best place is Pleasley Pit Country Park, a reclaimed old colliery site ▶

The limestone plateau grasslands between many of the dales are really areas of farmland. Viewed from the air the old, long, stone-walled fields produce a pattern and beauty of their own. In the bottom right a series of lead rakes can be seen as small grassy dimples. The lines of the old lead seams are now clear. It is here that the Derbyshire specialist, leadwort, a lead tolerant small, white flowered plant is found.

As summer passes through autumn the lives of many insects ends. This bee may have died on this twig before the first frost of the year has enshrined it with a coat of ice crystals.

A four spot orb spider waiting patiently among the rose hips. Chee Dale.

Dark green fritillaries are seldom still. This one is roosting on meadow cranesbill in Coombes Dale.

Globe flower in Cressbrook Dale. A member of the buttercup
family, globe flowers are not common in Derbyshire. They prefer
damp, cool soils often near trees or woodland edges and are
found in a small number of Derbyshire's Dales.

The brown argus is a member of the blue family of butterflies, though it isn't blue. There are two species of brown argus in the UK, the brown and northern brown. Derbyshire's arguses are the brown species though they oddly look like northern brown arguses!

Derbyshire's rivers, lakes and reservoirs

The limestone and gritstone uplands of Derbyshire are drained by some of England's finest rivers. The longest river in Derbyshire, at 80 kilometres, is the Derwent. Rising from the remote, wind-swept moors of Bleaklow and Howden, through the three reservoirs of Howden, Derwent and Ladybower it then charts a more leisurely path through Chatsworth. From there it journeys south to Matlock where Richard Arkwright harnessed its power until it finally joins the mighty Trent near Derby.

The Wye and Dove are two delightful limestone rivers that wend their way through some of the finest scenery in the UK. The Wye flows from Axe Edge Moor near Buxton through the limestone cliffed Chee Dale and Miller's Dale then via the wide waters of Water-cum-Jolly and Monsal Dale to Bakewell. The Dove also rises near Buxton as does the River Manifold.

Many of the limestone rivers disappear below ground for varying distances where they dissolve their way through the hard but soluble rock. Glacial melt waters thousands of years ago also dissolved the soluble limestone and produced the fabulous Blue John Caverns.

Some of the rivers such as the Lathkill are fed from aquifers below and are stable in temperature, rarely freeze over and, because of the natural filtering effect, are crystal clear and wildlife rich. Unfortunately drainage channels (soughs) from past lead mining have damaged some aquifers leaving a legacy of dry river beds. Recent work by the Environment Agency in Lathkill Dale is attempting to re-hydrate the river by pumping water into it once again and damming the sough. Dippers, kingfishers, grey wagtails, brown trout and numerous stunning invertebrates are here and should benefit from this vital work.

The Trent dominates the south of the county as it runs from west to east but in Derbyshire it is a shallow river of great importance for migratory birds. Sand martins nest in its earthy banks and fishermen compete with the cormorants and goosanders for the chub, tench and dace that swim in its clear water.

The eastern part of the county sees the River Rother, once heavily polluted, but now much cleaner, flowing north into South Yorkshire. Running almost along the Nottinghamshire - Derbyshire border is the River Erewash.

The age of canals left a visible mark across much of central England. The county boasts a stunning little canal at Cromford which was completed in 1798. The canal was intended to allow better transport links to Derby and Nottingham. The railways conspired to end the glory days of the canals and many fell into disrepair. From a wildlife point of view this was a huge bonus as weeds and sedges took root and russet brown water voles started to nibble their way through bank side vegetation in peace. Today the Cromford canal offers amazing wildlife opportunities coupled with a fascinating industrial heritage.

There are no significant, large natural lakes in Derbyshire but there are some fantastic stretches of open water. Many of these such as Woodhead, Staunton Harold, Linacre, Foremark, Ladybower and Carsington are reservoirs designed to supply our ever increasing thirst for clean water.

◀ A coot enduring a deluge.

Padley Gorge.

Others were created as landscape features such as the Emperor Lake, with its wintering goosanders, at Chatsworth and the long lake at Kedleston.

In the south of the county are flooded gravel workings. Here the shallow waters of places such as Hilton, Swarkestone and Willington offer superb wildlife watching with black-necked grebes, warblers, bitterns and water rails.

Derbyshire is a land-locked county and the ozone rich air of the sea is far away, yet the county does boast a plethora of maritime birds. Gravel workings can be viewed as mini-seas with sandy shores and oystercatchers and common terns now nest here.

Some of our gulls do not really deserve the name of seagull and none more so than the black-headed gull, an inland bird if there ever was one. They breed around the county with Woodhead reservoir having a gullery of over 100 pairs. Winter gull watching is a fascinating pastime and two reservoirs are particularly rich - Ogston and Carsington. Common terns and oystercatchers breed here and in winter great-northern divers and scaup put in fairly regular visits.

Some of the county's reservoirs are better for wildlife than others. The warmer and more nutrient rich waters of Carsington have a higher biodiversity than the northern acidic waters of the Longdendale reservoirs and the big three of Ladybower, Howden and Derwent. True, these may appear more dramatic but the cold waters are low in fish and there is little natural vegetation on the stony banks. However, fish are added to the waters of Ladybower to satisfy the demands of the fly fisherman and ospreys now regularly stop off for a few days to fish before moving north to the Lake District or Scotland. Ospreys breed just below Derbyshire, around Rutland Water, and with regular visits from these birds and passing migrants it cannot be too long before this charismatic bird nests in Derbyshire.

Despite problems with some of our native birds, there are some fantastic stories of in-comers to be told. Egyptian geese nested in Derbyshire for the first time in 2009 and showy exotic Mandarin ducks are spreading fast into many rivers and pools. Goosanders first bred in Derbyshire in 1982 and now are easy to see on many rivers and lakes. There are always a few pairs battling the swift waters of the Derwent near Hathersage. To watch a fishing goosander outsprint a trout like a deadly torpedo will take anyone's breath away. Red-breasted mergansers are still rare but an odd pair nests on a few of the bigger waters like Ladybower. In days past you had to travel to Scotland to see both our native sawbills, now you don't!

Unfortunately it is not all good news. Our clean water rivers like the Lathkill, with its unique trout should be chock-a-block full of native white-clawed crayfish. However, the release of signals, the North American crayfish brought over to farm and satisfy gourmet palates, has wrought havoc on our native species. Much is being done to reverse this invasion but it may always be an uphill one.

Kingfishers occur on many of Derbyshire's rivers though they are more abundant in the south where there are more small fish than in the northern, acidic rivers. This female was photographed as part of a long term project on the River Noe at Edale.

Mink, another North American farmed animal, also released with mind-numbing stupidity by those who should know better, is taking its toll on Ratty, our drop-dead gorgeous water vole. Oddly there may be a silver lining to this cloud from another of the great successes of modern conservation. As otters increase and holt up in our river banks it is thought that mink will decline, giving way to its larger British cousin and allowing Ratty to stage a come back.

Derbyshire boasts a good range of dragonflies and damselflies. Many of these are found in small, out-of-the way pools and ponds. On our moors some of these pools are home to the diminutive black darter dragonfly, azure, emerald and large red damsels and the much larger common hawker. Other places, at a lower elevation, are superb dragon sites. Pleasley Pit Country Park, on the eastern edge of the county, has a range of warm, shallow ponds that are home to a fantastic array of odonatas including emperors, four-spot chasers, black-tailed skimmers, common darters and, occasionally, the rare ruddy darter.

Female azure damselfly hiding behind a sedge. Pleasley Pit Country Park.

A four-Spot chaser emerging at Pleasley Pit Country Park. Dragonflies are creatures of two contrasting worlds. For most of their life they are ferocious predators living among the weeds at the bottom of shallow pools. Then in the summer the most spectacular change occurs. Leaving its watery world the nymph crawls up a sedge stem at dawn and transforms itself into a sublime creature of the air. This is a very vulnerable few hours as coots, mallards and moorhens roam the pool's edge looking for tasty snacks to get their day started. If they can avoid these, the young dragonfly, or teneral, seeks shelter in surrounding grasslands to mature before taking its place at the pool's edge once again.

An azure and large red damselfly roosting among the grasses on a dull day. Pleasley Pit Country Park.

Dippers are the quintessential birds of Derbyshire's river systems. Present all year round with their distinctive white bib and 'bobbing' mannerisms they epitomise the energy and life force of these shallow, fast flowing rivers. Whilst many of the rivers seem incredibly clean, all is not well with Derbyshire's dippers.

A few rivers, like the Bradford, are very popular and with increasing disturbance from walkers, dogs and photographers some stretches of river have lost their breeding dippers. As part of a long term study Sheffield University and Natural England have initiated a dipper project on some of the river systems.

There are many aspects of the project and one is to colour ring any adult dippers in the early spring before they start nesting. Colour rings are easily seen with binoculars and allow monitoring of dipper movements without having to catch or disturb the birds. Members of the public can help by phoning in any sightings of colour ringed birds.

The colours allow each dipper to be individually monitored. In some cases dippers breed in very public places where disturbance has caused them to repeatedly fail. To help them to nest away from these spots artificial nest tubes, effectively dipper bird boxes, have been constructed and placed into the river banks.

Derbyshire Custodians. Stephen Moores, head river keeper.

I guess your work may change through the year. Can you describe some of the major parts of your job? Yes, my work is very seasonal. During the autumn and winter we concentrate on maintaining the river system with jobs such as coppicing, tree planting and mending bridges. Also I monitor the trout redds, the shallow gravel beds that the fish spawn in, where I clear any weeds or silt. The trout season opens on the 18 March and the grayling season on the 1 July. They are different because they spawn at different times of the year. From then on I spend a lot of time patrolling the river and its wildlife, monitoring for pollution and clearing invasive plant species. I also spend time helping anglers who belong to the Litton and Cressbrook Fly Fishers Club plus those who fish with a day ticket. My knowledge of the river, where the fish lie and which insects are hatching is considerable as I have been a river keeper for over thirty years.

I have noticed that the river has felled trees and dead logs in it. Is there a purpose for these? That's a good question because I get a few comments from the public that the river is looking a little untidy yet these are vital for wildlife and the fish. In the past rivers were kept too clean and looked almost unnatural.

We now know that dead and even living trees felled into the river are very important. They are homes to many invertebrates, for example a couple of caddis fly larvae only live in submerged dead wood. They help to regulate the flow, protect fish-fry and all the invertebrates are invaluable for the fish and birds like dippers.

You mentioned that you carry out pollution monitoring. What does this mean? I check a number of sites along the Wye every year by kick sampling. Basically I catch all the invertebrates in each spot by disturbing the river bed and catching them in a net. A fairly simple calculation tells me how clean the water is. We are finding that the Wye is getting cleaner nearer to Buxton and that is really good for wildlife.

I have heard about stretches of the Wye that are called wild fishing. What does this mean? Yes, that's true. Large parts of the river have no fish added from bred stock and we don't allow any fish to be taken out. All the fish are wild and highly valued by fisherman. Less than 2% of all fish caught are actually taken out and these are from stretches that we stock. The Derbyshire Wye is the only UK river with a sustainable population of breeding rainbow trout. Many fishermen from all over the world come here to fish specifically for these rainbows.

Everyone has heard of poachers. Are they are a problem on the Wye? Definitely and they occupy a large part of my team's work. Some are relatively innocent but most are organised gangs who sell the fish for profit. I have to admit they are nothing like the 'sentimental' view of a poacher you see on TV and occasionally they resort to violence or threats.

What is your favourite wildlife experience? Oddly it's nothing to do with fish. In my spare time I ring wild birds under a BTO licence concentrating on dippers, grey wagtails and barn owls. I have put up over 50 barn owl nest boxes and finding one with chicks is one of my greatest wildlife experiences each year.

The River Wye flows peacefully through Miller's Dale.

We still think of harvest mice as tiny golden mammals of the wheat and barley fields but nothing is further from the truth. Modern cereal crops are a hostile place for this drop-dead-gorgeous little animal. Most of Derbyshire's prehensile-tailed rodents reside in wetland areas where plants like reed canary grass provide materials for the females to build their intricately woven ball-shaped nests.

Mallards grace many waters across the county. During the autumn reflections of sycamore leaves transforms the normally blue water into a stunning golden surface.

Grass snakes love water and regularly hunt frogs, newts and fish in
many of the ponds in the southern half of the county.

The Cromford Canal is home to little grebes.

Derbyshire Custodians. Shirley Cross, DWT volunteer

How did you get into working as a volunteer?
I originally started my voluntary work at Coombs Valley with the RSPB and later learnt a lot about surveying mammals with the Mammal Society. I then moved on to Derbyshire Wildlife Trust as the programme planner. When I retired in 1998 I had more time so I joined the mid-week volunteer's group. I learnt practical conservation skills including hedge laying, dry stone walling and scrub bashing on a wide range of the Trust's reserves. I really enjoyed this work but I wanted to have a more hands-on role with Derbyshire's wildlife so I started to learn the skills needed to do wildlife surveys.

You mentioned wildlife surveys. Which species have you worked with? I started with water voles and have worked surveying otters, small mammals, butterflies, wildfowl and plants. Most of my survey work has been with the Trust but I have surveyed for the BTO and Derbyshire Mammal Group as well. I enjoy the plant work but when it comes to grasses I do struggle with some identification!

Otters are known to have returned to Derbyshire. What experiences have you had with them so far?
I survey a number of rivers in the south of Derbyshire and I have regular beats on the Derwent, Amber, Trent and Ecclesbourne. I have six sites I survey each month and have done so for ten years. I think that on most of my sites any otter evidence is created by transitory otters that are passing through and not resident ones. The signs that I am looking for are spraint and footprints. The best so far has been the classic footprints and sliding mark made by a dog otter as it walked across a sand bar dragging its tail. My first sign was a spraint on the Derwent in 2000, the first evidence of an otter on my patch. It gave me an incredible thrill to find it.

I have heard of spraint. What exactly is it and how do you know it is from an otter?
Spraint is the polite term for otter pooh. It is easy to identify, when you pick it up it smells of sweet hay and is not fishy at all. When I break into it I look for fish scales and bones. I once found the bones of a bird. Fox and mink pooh are darker and very easy to tell from an otters. I wouldn't pick up mink pooh, it's disgusting!

Volunteering is clearly a huge commitment on your time, many might ask why you do it?
I love being outside and I want to be able to contribute to the knowledge of Derbyshire's wildlife. It is also a driving force to get me out and keep me fit. Sometimes it is incredibly rewarding such as when we find dormice during a survey at Chatsworth or a new spraint at a new site. Oddly I have never seen an otter in Derbyshire, I have to go to Mull for that.

What are your favourite wildlife experiences?
Simple - the return of swifts in May with their amazing flying skills and screams, hares boxing and the calls of curlews on the moors.

Otters have returned to Derbyshire and are spotted in many river systems. Derbyshire Wildlife Trust has received over 500 otter sightings in recent years.

Ospreys were known to breed in England hundreds of years ago. However, a constant level of persecution saw numbers dwindle until the last pair nested in Scotland in 1908. In the 1950's they re-colonised Scotland and have spread naturally south into Wales and the Lake District. In 1986 four young Scottish ospreys were translocated to Rutland Water with a total of 64 birds released up to 2001. Five pairs nested during 2010, producing twelve fledged young. Ospreys are seen regularly in Derbyshire and feed on many of the better fish stocked rivers and reservoirs and there is real optimism that they will breed in the very near future. In 2011, to give them a helping hand, artificial osprey platforms were erected in the south of the county at Carsington Water (above), Burnaston, Willington Gravel Pits, Drakelow and Besthorpe reserves.

Ponds fascinate us. We add them to gardens as features and to attract wildlife and as children we took great pleasure in dipping our nets to catch newts and beetles. When seen up close the small, often inconsequential, dark invertebrates take on great beauty and perhaps once again re-kindle those childhood experiences. From top left to bottom right. Great diving beetle adult, great diving beetle larvae, lesser water boatman and greater water boatman about to leave the pond.

Dew ponds like this one in Lathkill Dale are vital for wildlife. They were originally created by farmers to provide water for stock, though the water enters them by running off the surface after rain and not from heavy dews. They are often the only source of still, standing water for many miles and are vital for a great range of animals and plants. Many are used by great-crested newts to breed in. They are protected in Britain because we hold a significant proportion of Europe's population.

The larger rivers and Cromford canal are patrolled by the ultimate predator of the fish world, the pike. Even small ducklings and water voles are not safe from this impressive beast.

In winter many fish lie low and are fairly inactive because of the low temperatures. This tench is hiding in the weeds on the bottom of a pond. Its jewel-speckled eye catches a weak shaft of winter sun betraying its presence.

For a land-locked county Derbyshire can boast an amazing number of sea birds. Some like this arctic tern just pass through on their way north. Others like common terns, shelduck, cormorants and oystercatchers are established breeding birds.

Bitterns are related to herons but are far rarer and more secretive. In the last few years more are overwintering on some of our reedy pools like those at Willington gravel pits.

River Lathkill.

Water shrews are ferocious little predators that are just as
at home hunting in the water as they are patrolling the wet
banks of rivers and streams across Derbyshire.

The future for Derbyshire

The new big picture

Saving plants and animals that are on the brink of extinction seems an obvious thing to do and we are familiar with the term conservation but how is it actually carried out? Understanding why something is becoming rare is a good start though the reason is not always obvious. Years ago we tended to concentrate on the actual animal or plant but as our knowledge of habitats and ecology developed we switched to a more enlightened view and saw that all species are interconnected and that the immediate habitat was the place to focus attention.

We saw the answer in creating nature reserves, little islands of habitat that become an oasis for that particular plant or animal. Many were very small and isolated and we quickly realised that they were vulnerable and that highways of connectivity were needed. These could be simple things such as rivers or hedgerows, the transport infrastructure of the natural world. Even so there were often miles of sterile countryside, or urban environments, that separated these vital reserves.

Add to this many other threats - new homes to be built in the countryside, increases in flooding and the insidious presence of global warming - it is easy to see that we need a new way of joined - up thinking.

Living Landscapes and the RSPB's Futurescapes are exactly that. They are a holistic way of looking at the countryside, viewing it as a whole. They not only focus on the small reserves, although these still remain the jewels in the crown, but also on the entire environment - the crown that holds the jewels safe.

The creators of, and driving force behind Living Landscapes are the Wildlife Trusts of the UK. They have a clear vision – 'in restoring, recreating and reconnecting wildlife-rich spaces in rural and urban areas by working in partnership with local communities, landowners, schools and businesses. We want wildlife to thrive, to disperse and re-colonise our landscape so future generations can encounter, experience and enjoy our natural heritage.'

The core of every Living Landscape or Futurescape is its jewels, the nature reserves and protected sites. Then comes the interconnected part, to join up these sites with rivers, hedges and grass banks. These will allow wildlife, including plants, to travel more effectively across their environment.

Lastly comes the infilling bit, to improve the poorer, less wildlife-attractive areas within the Living Landscape. This is where landowners, including farmers, have a vital part to play. It may simply be small changes in farming to increase wildflower diversity, or managing town parks for nesting birds or roosting bats, as in Derby or Alfreton.

There is also another way of looking at our countryside and green spaces - what they actually provide for us, ecological services. Spending time with wildlife can decrease stress

◄ Lime-spec pug hiding on a silver birch.

Wyver Lane Pools nature reserve near Belper. An important
wetland site for birds in the Lower Derwent Valley.

and improve well - being. Our countryside also cleans our water, woods filter air pollution, boglands trap carbon and farms provide food. Living Landscapes and Futurescapes recognise these vital services along with the character of the landscape and the wildlife that shares our world. Ambitious and inspirational without doubt!

Natural England's Nature Improvement Areas

Initiated in 2011, 12 pilot schemes across Britain follow the same philosophy as Living Landscapes. In Derbyshire there is one scheme, 'Dark Peak: public and private lands partnership'. Three core areas of 5,800 hectares will hopefully witness extensive moorland restoration, woodland planting and increasing wildlife-rich grasslands. This is a government funded project with the RSPB as a lead partner. It initially focuses on public owned, National Trust and United Utilities land in Longdendale, the High Peak Estate and East and Big moors. If the funding can produce tangible results the hope is that the initiative will encourage privately owned estates to become involved and new Nature Improvement Areas to be designated in the future.

Derbyshire Living Landscapes are: -

The Derwent Valley and Derby. This large and ambitious scheme stretches over 88 km from the moors and ancient woodlands around Ladybower through the heart of Derbyshire to Derby. Its primary aim is to restore, extend and link together existing habitats whilst safeguarding and restoring the Derwent Valley Mills World Heritage site.

The Trent Valley. The Trent is southern Derbyshire's dominant landscape feature. It is an incredibly important natural highway for wildlife. The aim is to enhance and reconnect the river, floodplain, wildlife and local communities. Derbyshire Wildlife Trust has several reserves like Barton Pool and Willington Gravel Pits here. Key species are water voles, grass snakes, black poplar trees (Derbyshire contains 20% of Britain's total), wetland breeding birds and winter wildfowl.

The River Erewash. This largely urban area with wetlands on the Derbyshire border has suffered from extensive coal mining. The river and Erewash canal are important for native crayfish, water voles and grass snakes. DWT's newest reserve at Shipley is within this exciting project.

Limestone Dales and River Wye. Beginning close to Buxton, this encompasses incredible scenery and wildlife - rich dales like Chee Dale and Monk's Dale. These dales have superb plants such as limestone fern, mossy saxifrage and moonwort. The River Wye is a stunning river, wildlife-rich with invertebrates and a healthy wild trout population.

Linacre and northern Peak fringe including Chesterfield. The focus within this Living Landscape is on the decline of semi-natural grasslands on the fringe of the Peak Park.

Dove Valley. Running down the West of the county the River Dove is a natural corridor for many plants and animals.

Rose End Meadows and Carsington Meadows. Orchid-rich grasslands feature heavily in this scheme.

Rother and Doe Lea including Bolsover. An area of past industrialisation, this is one of the newest Living Landscapes in Derbyshire.

Sand martins are the first birds of the swallow family to return in spring. Colonies exist in the banks of many of Derbyshire's larger rivers like the Derwent at Chatsworth and the Trent. Other colonies are found at Staveley Works, Whitwell Quarry and Derby Loco Works.

Derbyshire Biodiversity Action Plans

Buzz words abound in modern society and come and go with monotonous regularity. Occasionally one appears that has real meaning and sums up what it's all about. Biodiversity is certainly not a new term but it has taken on a fresh meaning since the Rio Earth Summit in 1992. Biodiversity is a neat term that expresses the richness of the natural world. It simply means the number of different species in any one place - the more species, the higher the biodiversity. In modern terms the word now includes the variety of different habitats and ecological processes (things like food webs) which interlock all species into one complex dynamic system.

We use biodiversity to drive conservation forward and draw up our plans for the future - we call these biodiversity action plans (BAPS). There are two local BAPS for Derbyshire which identify the key habitats and species that need most conservation work. They are the Peak District BAP and the Lowland Derbyshire BAP (which includes part of the National Forest BAP).

Each BAP sets out the reasons why the habitat or species needs consideration (if known, what are the causes of its decline?) and an action plan that we should be implementing to reduce the threats in order to increase that habitat or species. The work on the ground and the creation and management of the BAPS in Derbyshire is carried out by an amalgamation of many groups so that a holistic approach is adopted. Key players in our BAPS are Natural England, Derbyshire Wildlife Trust, local Councils, the Forestry Commission, the National Trust, the RSPB and the Peak Park Authority.

In the Peak District BAP there are fifteen habitat and seven species BAPS. The Lowland Derbyshire BAP is newer, having been re-written in 2011. Instead of identifying separate habitats it seeks to utilise more modern thinking that focuses on the character of the landscape as well as the different habitats and species. It has its roots in the same philosophy as the Living Landscapes initiatives. The Lowland Derbyshire BAP identifies eight larger areas, known as Action Areas.

The BAPS seek to move in three ways – initially with the conservation of any remaining habitat, followed by the restoration of any damaged parts and ultimately the recreation (or simply creation) of new habitat.

The larger habitat BAPS in the Peak District BAP are: -

Upland ash woods. These are found in the White Peak on the sides of many of the dales and Via Gellia near Cromford. These Peak ash woods are the largest examples of this habitat in Britain and are not only of UK significance but of importance in a European context.

Upland oak-birch woodlands. The majority of these are found on valley sides in the Dark Peak. This was probably the dominant woodland type across much of northern Derbyshire before pre-historic man. They have suffered a significant decline in extent over the last 100 years and this habitat type is of national importance.

Absent as a breeding bird for over a 100 years, red kites now often play in the air above Derbyshire. In 2011 a pair were regularly spotted above the same wood in the south of the county throughout the breeding season. Hopefully, over the next 20 years this will become a common breeding raptor in south and central Derbyshire.

154

Limestone Dales. The dales have their own BAP because they contain many small habitats within them - grasslands (calcareous and neutral), ash woods, scrub, scree slopes and cliffs. Each has its own unique assemblage of species.

Traditional hay meadows. These have a rich mix of wild flowers and insects and are one of the fastest declining habitats in the UK. In Derbyshire they have declined by over 70% in the last twenty five years.

Lead rakes. Chains of small hollows were created by the mining of lead from as long ago as the Roman period. The lead rakes have a unique group of plants including spring sandwort (known locally as leadwort) and mountain pansy that have evolved to survive the high amounts of the toxic heavy metal in the soil.

Ponds and standing open water. There are somewhere around 3000 ponds in Derbyshire with a significant number being dew ponds. These occur mainly in the White Peak where they form superb habitats of open standing water in a landscape where it is rare.

Blanket bog. There are significant amounts of this habitat in Derbyshire and the Peak District. Whilst it is extensive locally it is of global significance with Britain containing about 15% of the planet's blanket bogs. They form in upland areas of high rainfall and peat forms beneath the sphagnum mosses. Most of the blanket bog is found in the north of the county with Howden Moors and Eastern Moors being notable areas but there are also smaller patches in the south at Warslow Moors.

Heather moorland. The defining habitat of the northern part of Derbyshire though there are significant acreages in the south around the Roaches.

The eight Action Areas in the Lowland Derbyshire BAP are: -

Magnesian Limestone. Running from Shirebrook in the south, via Bolsover to Clowne in the north, this action area is characterised by rolling farmland dissected by narrow river valleys and gorges and includes Cresswell Crags, Pleasley Pit Country Park and Steetley Quarries. Fields with hawthorn hedges, grasslands and woodlands all feature. Farmland birds are vital and the area is one of the last in Derbyshire to have breeding corn bunting and turtle dove.

Rother and Doe Lea Valleys. In the northern part of the Derbyshire coal fields this area has a broad range of habitats including farmland, river valleys, mixed and ancient woodlands plus meadows and heaths.

Peak Fringe. This is a well wooded, farming landscape bordering the east of the Peak Park and running from Dronfield in the north through Belper in the south to Ashbourne in the west. The area includes the river valleys of the Amber, Derwent and Ecclesbourne. This areas vision is ' A pastoral undulating landscape dominated by wildlife rich ancient woodland, interspersed with upland heath and small flower filled fields bounded by dry stone walls and species - rich hedgerows.'

Great-crested newts are protected in Britain by the Wildlife and Countryside Act. Derbyshire has some very important sites for this, the largest of our three newt species. Dew ponds in the White Peak and ponds in many action areas such as Claylands, are vital breeding sites ▶

Smooth newts are smaller than great-crested newts and are far more widespread across the whole of the county. In spring they return to their breeding ponds where the males grow a beautiful crest along their back.

Erewash Valley. In the south Derbyshire coal fields this area is mainly mixed farming with river valleys, meadows and woodlands. Its vision is 'A rich diversity of wetland habitats linked by a river channel restored to a more natural condition, and flanked by farmland rich in wildlife.'

Claylands. The large area between Ashbourne and the city of Derby is a pastoral landscape with some important wetland habitats lying on glacial clays with small, flower-rich fields and many hedgerows.

Derby. The city of Derby is 75% urban with the River Derwent providing an important wildlife corridor through the city. There are many remnant habitats within its green spaces. Derby's area vision is 'An area where all people have access to and value their wildlife rich environment close to where they live and work. Open land will be sustainably managed for people and wildlife, new built development will play a part in delivering new and enhanced habitats.'

Trent and Dove Valleys. Following the flood plains of the Trent and Dove this long action area is one of grassland habitats with flood meadows and hawthorn hedges. Wet woodland and scrub along with important wildlife - rich gravel pits also occur.

National Forest area. Situated in the South of Derbyshire with Swadlincote at its heart this area is complex and mainly agricultural with many fragmented woodlands including Calke Abbey. There are some small river corridors and fields with hawthorn hedges. The vision for the future is 'A managed working landscape, where existing habitats are buffered and linked with new habitats to create strong habitat corridors. Hedgerows especially are strengthened where they form vital wildlife corridors.'

Toad patrols are vital to help the warty amphibians cross roads in the breeding season.

Biodiversity recognises all life forms and reminds us just how important they all are, even the humble woodlouse. Woodlice are vital animals in the recycling of dead wood and vegetation and are covered by armoured plates like tiny armadillos.

The sun blazes through the miniature forest of lichens growing on a limestone wall. When viewed closely they resemble a fairy-tale world of castles and turrets floating amongst the mist in a surreal kingdom.

Derbyshire Custodians. Nick Moyes, the Derby Cathedral peregrines.

Many people think that they feed mainly on city pigeons. Is this true?
It would seem the obvious thing to eat but the birds do leave the city and hunt over a wider area. The most amazing thing is that city peregrines often hunt at night and feed on migrating birds that follow the nearby River Derwent corridor. We know the light produced by Derby at night actually helps them to spot and hunt birds. We've even captured rare video evidence proving this. The adults have caught 50 different species of birds including terns, kingfishers and woodcock plus 12 species of waders. It seems they don't prey on any one species but sample the many different types of birds that occur around and over Derby.

In terms of the peregrines the project is amazingly successful but has it attracted the attention of the people of Derby?
Definitely. This is probably its greatest success. We run 'Watch Points' with telescopes where we help people see the birds for real. We also have three webcams on the nest and this attracts up to half a million hits in a year. We have lots of locals logging on to follow the birds but we've also an amazing international audience. We even have one person on Christmas Island who loyally follows Derby's peregrines! We have a Flickr site and 50 video clips on Youtube tube as well.

I read that the peregrines first nested in 2006 but that they needed a helping hand. How did that come about?
Yes, that's true. Two adult birds had been around the previous year but we couldn't imagine where they might nest on the cathedral because there were simply no ledges big enough. I am a keen mountaineer, as is my friend, another Nick, but he is also a joiner. So he agreed to construct a huge nest platform which we would fit ourselves by abseiling down the cathedral. Everything was ready in March, but then the weather turned really bad and we couldn't install it until April 5th. We thought this would be too late for them to use but the male was perching on it within days, and a few weeks later we saw the female incubating eggs there. They raised those chicks successfully and have done so every year since, producing 19 fledged young in seven years.

Which part of this fabulous project gives you the greatest satisfaction?
Simple - the huge response from other people, especially from those who had no real interest in wildlife before. It's their sense of discovery about what's in their city - the fastest bird in the world. That's brilliant! Quite a few have gone on to become truly fascinated by the natural world around them. The birds are not bothered about us but they create such a fantastic response in so many people - that is my greatest buzz!

Derby Cathedral peregrines is a project championed by Derby Wildlife Trust, Derby Museum and Derby Cathedral.

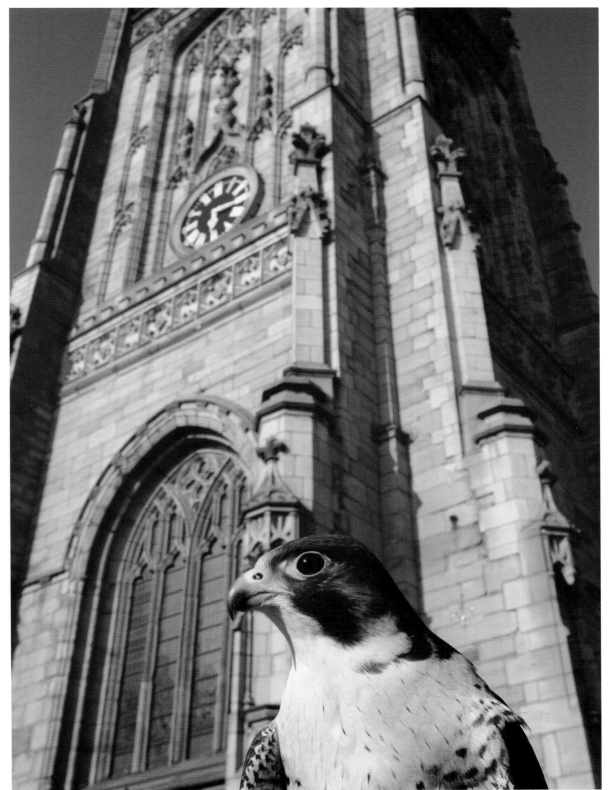

A water vole munches on one of its
favourite spring snacks - willow catkins.

Eight Derbyshire species have have their own Biodiversity Action Plan (BAP)

Water vole. This is possibly the fastest declining mammal in the UK with estimates of a 90% reduction in range and numbers since 1945. In Derbyshire there are some very good colonies and it is fairly widespread with over 180 km of occupied river and canal side habitat. There is a lot of evidence to suggest that it has declined dramatically in some areas of the White Peak though its numbers in the Dark Peak are higher than first thought and probably stable. Water voles occur in many of Derbyshire's river systems with strong populations in the headwaters of the Derwent, Dove and Etherow. They are found down much of the Derwent, Manifold, Dane and Wye, in many dales like Bradford and Lathkill Dale and along the Chesterfield and Cromford canals. The population in Derbyshire is considered a stronghold in the UK.

Water voles are large aquatic rodents with a lovely russet fur that live along river systems. They are as happy swimming in the water as they are grazing the bank side vegetation. The distinctive 'plop' as one dives headfirst into the safety of the water is often the first indication that they are present. With a little patience they are not difficult to watch. Other signs of their presence will be small grazed areas like mini lawns on the bank and collections of droppings at water level, perhaps on a stone or piece of mud, which form their latrines.

Conservation of this super animal takes many forms - controlling mink numbers, cleaning up polluted waters and protecting and re-vegetating banks to provide cover and food, plus allowing isolated populations the ability to meet

and mix. In some areas water voles are bred in captivity and released into habitats once they have been improved or recreated. In the last two years 10 km of habitat have been improved by removing Himalayan balsam.

Curlew. As winter retreats and the cold winds and sleet showers head further north the moorland waders return to breed. There is no more evocative sound than the long, liquid notes of a returning curlew to the brown, bleak moors. It is the sound that symbolises the passing of the dormant season into one of life and hope.

Curlew numbers are fairly stable in Derbyshire. Their strongholds are the heather moors of the North and those on the Staffordshire border but they also breed at lower elevations and are found throughout many of the farming areas in the south. There is some evidence that numbers have declined in pastures that have been improved, for example fields that have been drained or converted to silage. It is thought that the increase in crows in key wader breeding habitats is depleting curlew numbers due to higher egg and chick predation.

Derbyshire's population is roughly 1000 pairs which is about 2 to 3% of the UK total. The curlew is the UK's largest wader and returns to Derbyshire in the spring to lay its four well camouflaged, large eggs in a rudimentary nest on the ground. Only one brood is reared per year and the youngsters leave with the adults in the late summer, returning to the marshes and mudflats of the coast to overwinter.

The evocative call of the curlew returning to the moors and upland hill farms in spring is one of Derbyshire's most magical sounds.

Conservation is geared around protecting or restoring areas where curlews nest. Examples include recreating hay meadows near Edale and re-wetting soils in compacted fields at Padley. The RSPB have produced a curlew friendly farming leaflet to give to landowners and, where possible, will provide help and advice.

Lapwing. As the curlew returns to the moors so the lapwing reclaims the rough pasture fields in the early spring. Lapwings are often locally known as peewits or green plovers. Their numbers across England, including Derbyshire, have plummeted by over 50% in the last 40 years. Fields that once had the air above them cleaved with the tumbling flight and calls of courting lapwings are now eerily silent.

In the past, lapwings bred right across Derbyshire extending from lowland to upland farms. The Edale valley, much of the White Peak and the Trent Valley have lost most of their colonies. Most are now restricted to upland farms on the edges of moors in the north of the county. The key reason for this loss is changes in farming practice on wet, rough grassy fields.

Lapwings lay four eggs which they incubate for four weeks. During this period they need the grass to grow slowly and not be disturbed by farm machinery. Once the chicks hatch they are able to run with their parents in only a few hours. The parents then lead them to areas of wet soil and rough grass where there are plenty of invertebrates to feed on. The loss of these invertebrate-rich, damp grasslands and slow growing grasses like those in old hay meadows has contributed to the bird's decline.

The key factor in helping lapwings is to recreate those grassy, rough fields with damp, invertebrate-rich soils. This may often mean a loss of income for Derbyshire's farmers but there are a number of agri-environmental schemes like Countryside Stewardship which can compensate for this.

Twite. A birding term that is often used, and is very apt at times, is LBJ, or little brown job. It depicts accurately, though a little condescendingly, a number of small, innocuous birds that live in the UK. Moorlands have two, one many of us are familiar with, the meadow pipit, and the other, rarely seen now, the twite.

Sometimes known as the mountain linnet, the twite was common right across most of northern Derbyshire's moorlands. It has a distinctive song and nests in bracken and heather in colonies. The adults feed exclusively on wild seeds in the damp, flower-rich fields that border the moors they breed on. It is the loss of these fields which have been improved with chemicals and drainage that has seen twite numbers plummet.

Twite are now almost exclusively restricted to the northern part of the Dark Peak around Digley, Winscar and Butterley reservoirs and Wessenden. This population is the most southerly European population of twite and is separate from the larger Scottish population.

Twite numbers in England are only about 1500 pairs and the North Peak population is very significant. They are brown finches that breed late in the spring, often not laying their four or five blue speckled eggs until June. The nest is hidden

Lapwing numbers have tumbled alarmingly in the last few decades. Hopefully all the hard work now being done to provide fields with the right blend of invertebrates will see this amazing bird becoming a common sight across most of the county again.

in heather or bracken and can be difficult to find. The easiest way to locate them is by learning their song and spotting them as they feed or fly across the moor.

The main conservation efforts are directed at maintaining and recreating traditional hay meadows, both in areas with good twite populations and those that have lost their breeding birds. For a number of years twite have been artificially fed to support winter numbers.

White-clawed crayfish. Bubbling clear streams are still the norm in Derbyshire, they look clean and alive but not all is well below the surface of many. During the summer the gravelly bottoms should be patrolled by the lobster of the freshwater, the native white-clawed crayfish. However, this is not the case in many river systems.

Our desire for exotic foods like crayfish tails saw huge numbers of foreign crayfish imported into England to be bred for the table. The main species chosen was the North American signal crayfish. Anything held in captivity escapes eventually, often with the helping hand of a well meaning, if misinformed human. Signals now crawl across many of Derbyshire's stream beds. They are larger than the native and out-compete them for food and breeding holes in the soft river banks.

Unfortunately there is an even more insidious menace, the signals carry a disease - crayfish plague. This is a fungal infection that signals are partly immune to but not our native crayfish, which rapidly disappear when signals work into a river system.

Once common in virtually all the limestone rivers of the southern part of Derbyshire, native crayfish have disappeared from virtually all the rivers like the Lathkill and Bradford. They are now only found in a couple of spots on the Dove and Manifold. This huge decline is mirrored across much of England.

White-clawed crayfish are found in the more acidic waters of north Derbyshire but the lack of calcium in the water means numbers are always lower here and they are naturally scarcer. An ark site (a safe refuge) for white claws has been set up near Chesterfield.

Conservation is focussed on a number of fronts. Where possible signal crayfish are removed from rivers but this is often virtually impossible to implement. Where white-claws

Hedgehogs are loved by virtually everyone yet they are suffering in our modern world. We can all do our bit in Derbyshire to try to make our gardens as hog friendly as possible by reducing chemical use, leaving piles of leaves to help hibernating hogs and letting the snails and slugs take their own chances!

168

have disappeared captive breeding and release can be tried, as is being pioneered on the River Lathkill. General river management to improve conditions for crayfish will include bank work and pollution reduction.

Appleyard's feather moss. This delightful moss is found at only eight sites in the limestone dales of Derbyshire. It was once thought to only occur in England but a couple of other colonies have been found in Europe. In Britain the eight Derbyshire populations represent 80% of the UK total and the majority of the global total.

The moss has very precise habitat requirements, it is found at the base of limestone cliffs under overhangs which protect it from rain and wind. Its main threats include scrub growing and shading it, collectors who target rare mosses and climbers and people who inadvertently damage it.

The main conservation strategies focus on protection of all the known sites and research to find if any other sites exist. To safeguard any very rare species it is often desirable to have colonies maintained in captivity so that if the worst happens there are plants available to re-introduce later. It may be possible to introduce the moss to other areas that are ideal but at the moment do not have viable colonies.

Derbyshire feather moss. The only known colony of this moss globally is found at one site in the White Peak. Derbyshire feather moss is an aquatic species that grows in the water. Little is known about it and its relationship to other feather mosses appears confused. Since it only occurs at one site it is safe to say it is naturally very rare. The main

conservation strategies look at protecting it at this one site as well as maintaining two 'captive' populations.

Oak polypore. A special fungus found on old oak trees. Calke and Kedleston are two old parklands where this nationally rare fungus can be found. Oak polypore is associated with old oak trees and the Great Trees of Derbyshire project helped to identify as many veteran trees as possible. It is these veteran oaks that allow the fungi to survive.

White-clawed crayfish

References.

Birds of Derbyshire, R.A. Frost, 1978
Derbyshire Wildlife Trust, Biodiversity Action Plans, reports.
Derbyshire Ornithological Society annual bird reports
Endangered Wildlife in Derbyshire, T. Elkington, A Wilmot, 1996
The Peak District, K.C. Edwards, 1964
Wild flowers and other Plants of the Peak District, P. Anderson D. Shimwell, 1981

www.chatsworth.org/
www.derbyshirebiodiversity.org
www.derbyshireuk.net/people.html
www.derbyshireos.org.uk/index.asp
www.derbyshirewildlifetrust.org.uk
www.irenebrierton.co.uk/Badger%20Group.htm
www.kew.org/science/sainsbury.html
www.naturalengland.org.uk/ourwork/conservation
www.nationaltrust.org.uk
www.nationalforest.org/
www.peakdistrictonline.co.uk
www.peakdistrict.gov.uk/
www.peakdistrictinformation.com
www.rspb.org.uk/futurescapes/
www.rspb.org.uk/Images/PeakMalpractice_tcm9-132666.pdf
www.wildlifewatch.org.uk/Where-you-live/East-Midlands/Derbyshire
en.wikipedia.org/wiki/Derbyshire + people
www.wildlifetrusts.org

The following images were taken under controlled conditions, P16, 25, 34, 35, 37, 44, 82, 89, 94, 132, 137, 142, 161(RH only)

Sometimes we may focus too much on rare species. It is often a good idea to remind ourselves how much wildlife actually lives alongside us. Wild Derbyshire not only occurs on the moors and in the woods but also in our towns and gardens. Often derelict land may appear barren and lacking in wildlife but a second glance will reveal an excellent range of plants and animals such as this robin living around an abandoned old hut.

Originally from Manchester, Paul moved to Sheffield in the late 1970's to study Natural Environmental Science at Sheffield University. He then trained to be a teacher and he worked as an Environmental Science lecturer for over twenty years until he moved into wildlife photography full time.

Today Paul travels around the world but he is never happier than when he is working in Derbyshire. The demands on the photographer are harder, the rewards greater.

Paul hopes that through his photography he can elevate the status of wildlife and its issues in the public's eye and provide a firm platform of images to complement the conservation of Britain's wildlife.

He is the species staff photographer for Natural England in Derbyshire and the Peak District and he writes a monthly article about local wildlife for Derbyshire Life. He has been Amateur Photographer's Wildlife Master-class expert and his images and articles feature regularly in BBC Wildlife, Birdwatching, Birdwatch, Outdoor Photographer and Natural World.

His international awards include specially commended in the Wildlife Photographer of the Year, category winner in the European Wildlife Photographer of the Year and highlighted in Glanslichter International Wildlife Photography Competition. In all three years since its launch he has had images in the final of the British Wildlife Photography Awards and has been highly commended.

Paul's work is represented by a number of leading nature photographic libraries in the UK including NPL, FLPA and the RSPCA.

www.paulhobson.co.uk

Acknowledgements

The inspiration for this book has relied on the help of a great many people, too many to name in full. To those who I have left out, my apologies. To one and all, my huge thanks for all your help, access to land or guidance. It has meant a great deal, even when I ignored it or needed to be persuaded that I was on the wrong track!

Mike Ashton	Phil Bowler	John Bradwell
Carol Cranfield	Steve Colmer	Lee Davies
Diane Gilder	Danny Green	Russell Hague
Paul Hallam	Joy Hales	Mark Hamblin
Jenny Harris		Robert Hawkesworth
Andy Heath	Jim Hodson	Mike Innerdale
Edwin Kats	Mike Lane	John Lintin-Smith
Geoff Mawson	Robin Metcalfe	Phil Newman
Andy Parkinson	Ian Shaw	Andy Smith

Mark Sisson   Paul Stafford   Graham Thorpe
Fran and David Tomalin
Russel Wade   Jamie Walker   Terry Whitaker
all the Custodians
Derbyshire Wildlife Trust
Derbyshire Ornithological Society
and of course Mike Muddiman, without whom many of the images and much of this book would not have existed.

And lastly to Judy, my other half, who has had to put up with so much - though it was all good!